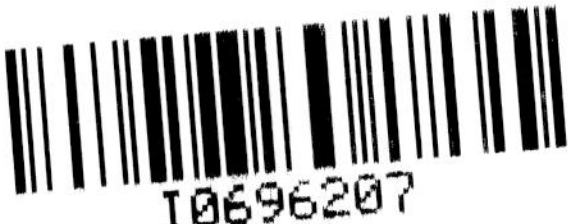

I am grateful to God for everything! And I believe that the meaning of life is to make sense of other lives. C.A., you are the meaning of my life.
Lov U

Jéssica Bragança
2024

This Book Belongs to:

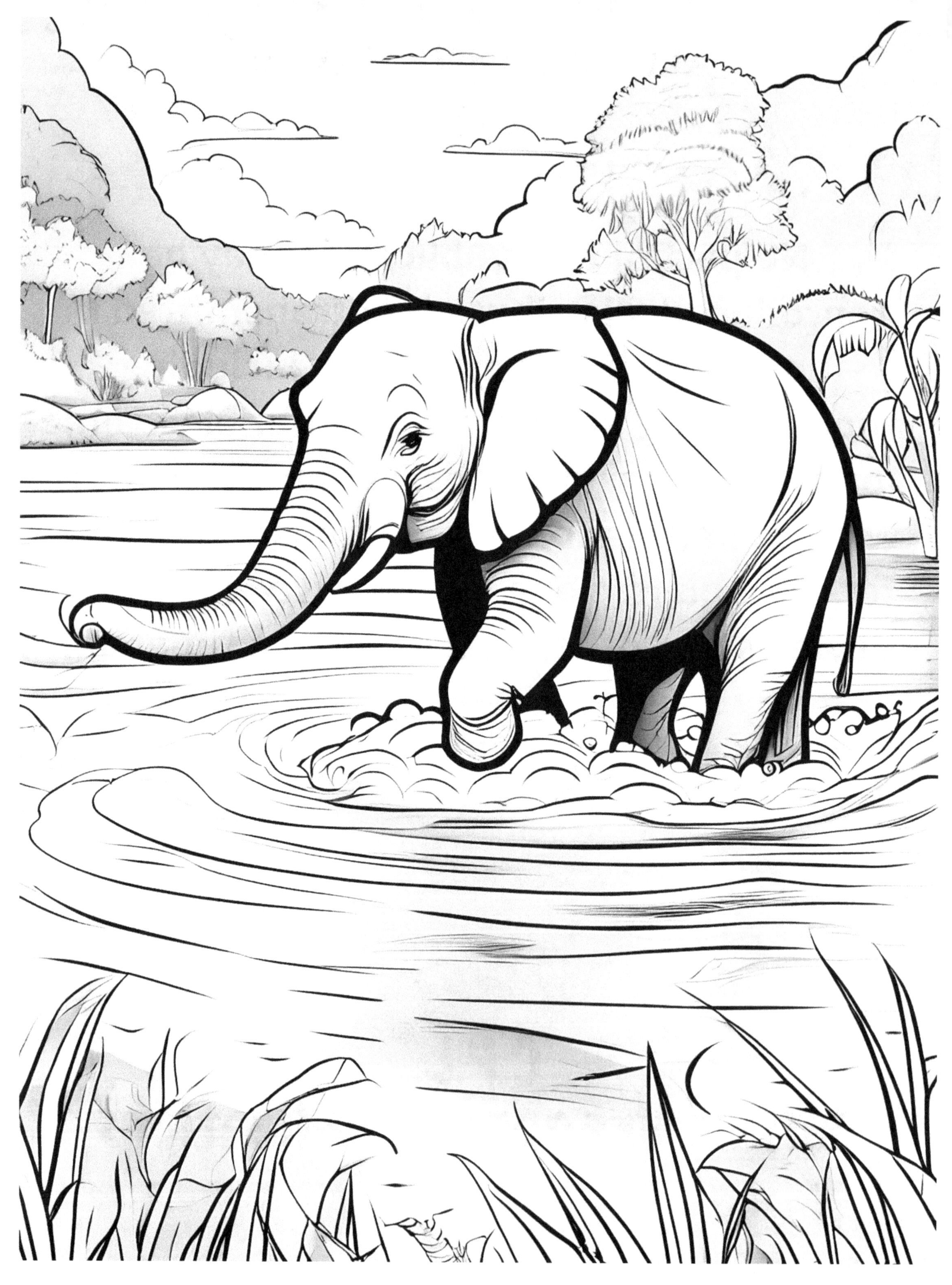

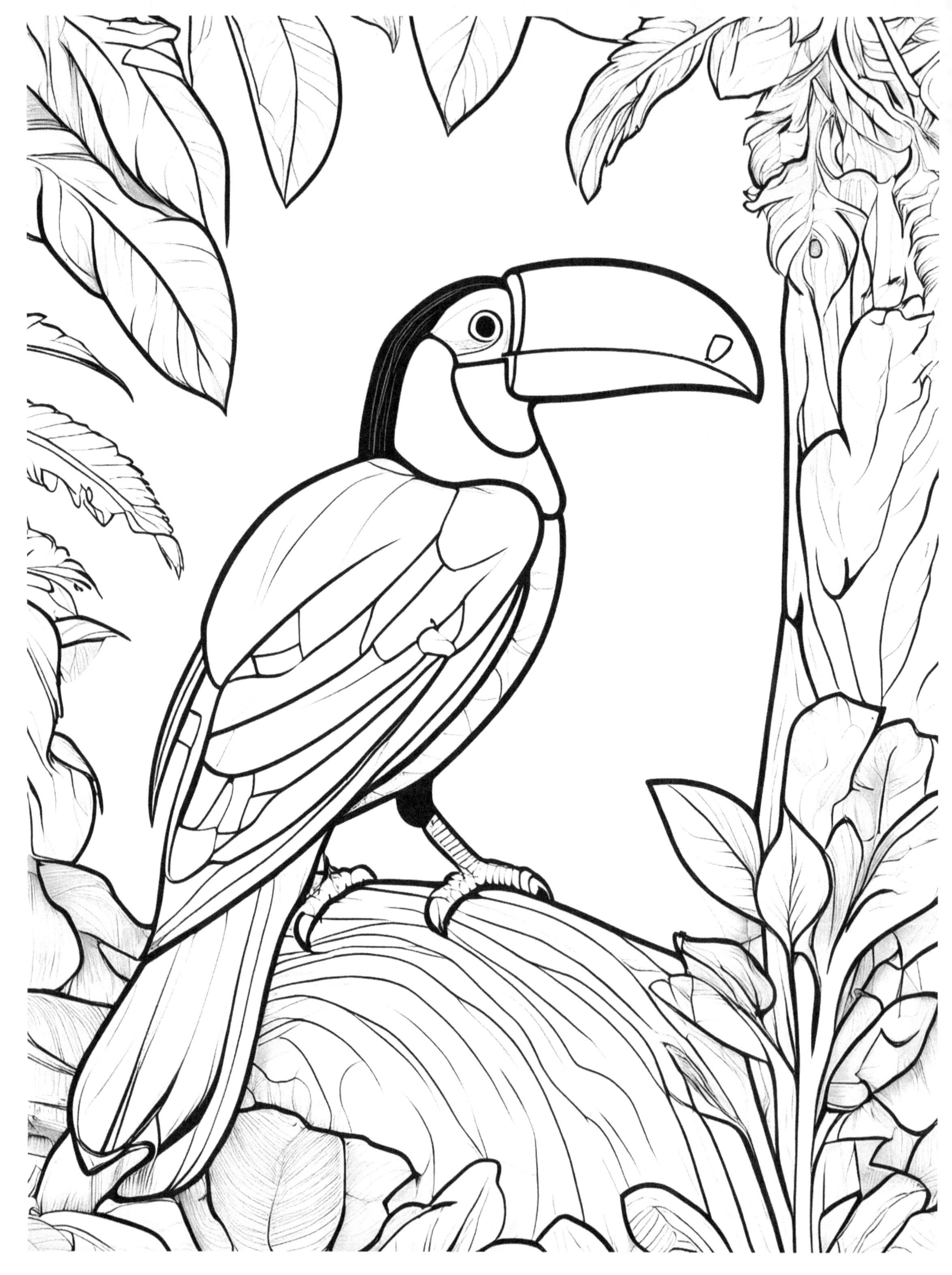

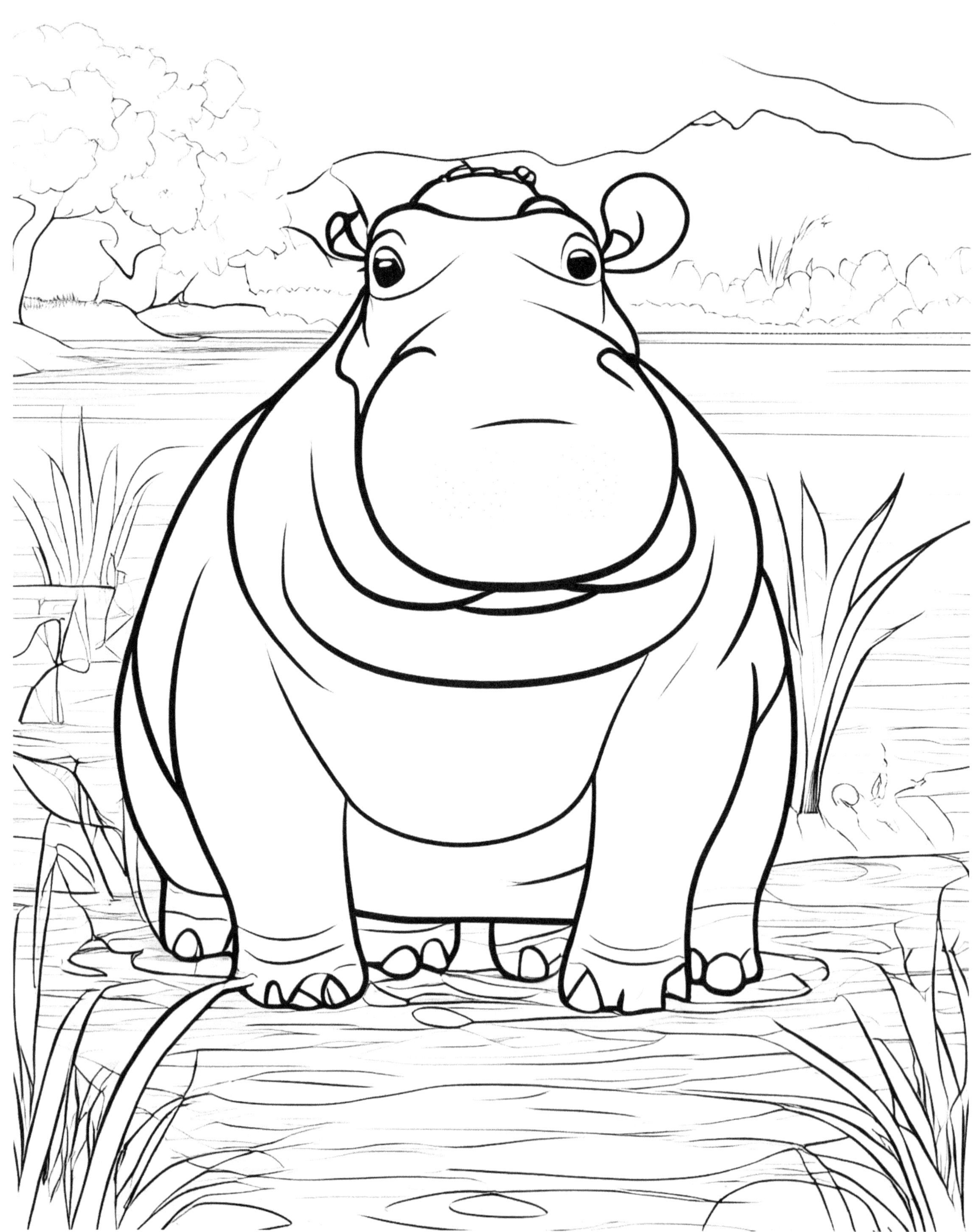

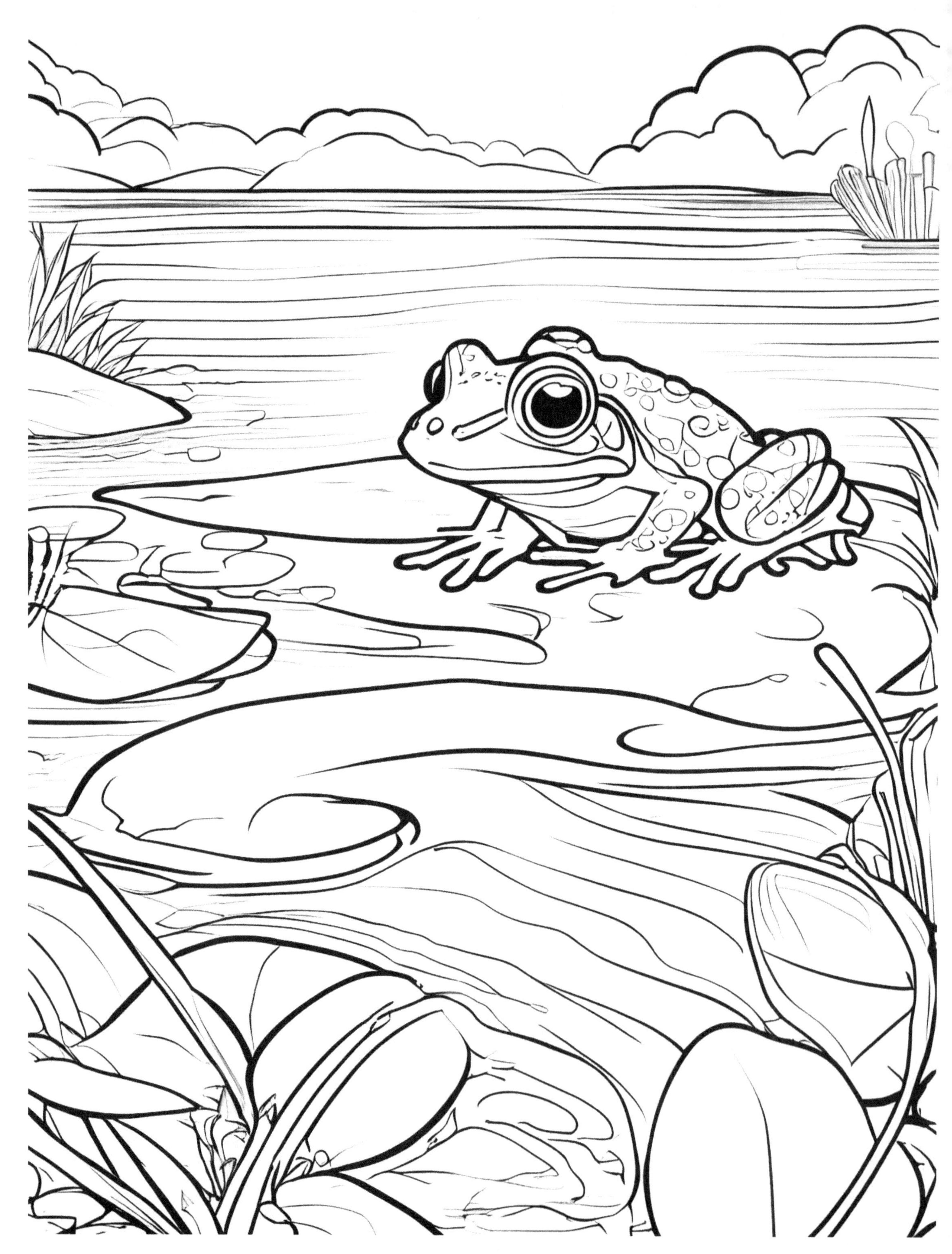

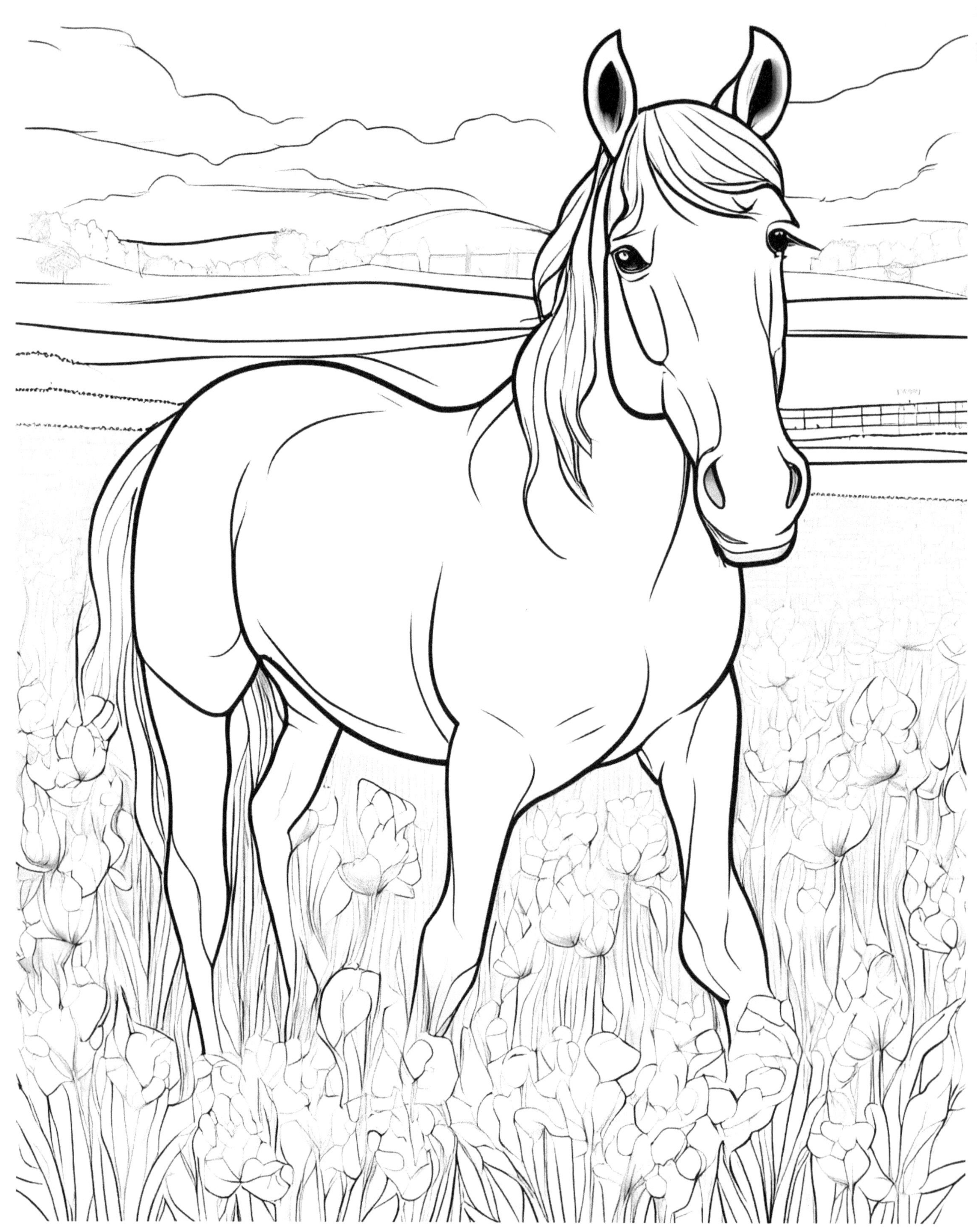

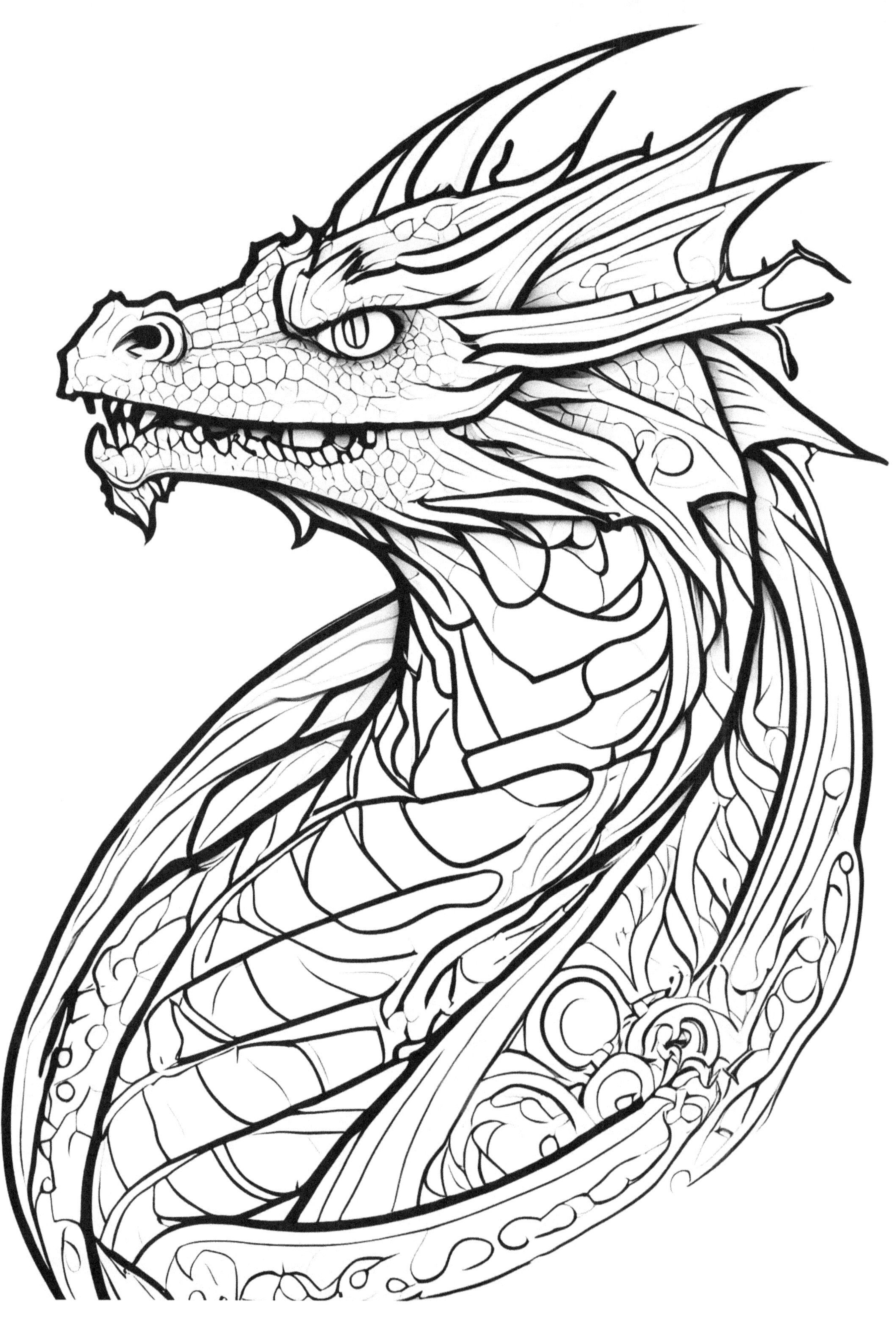

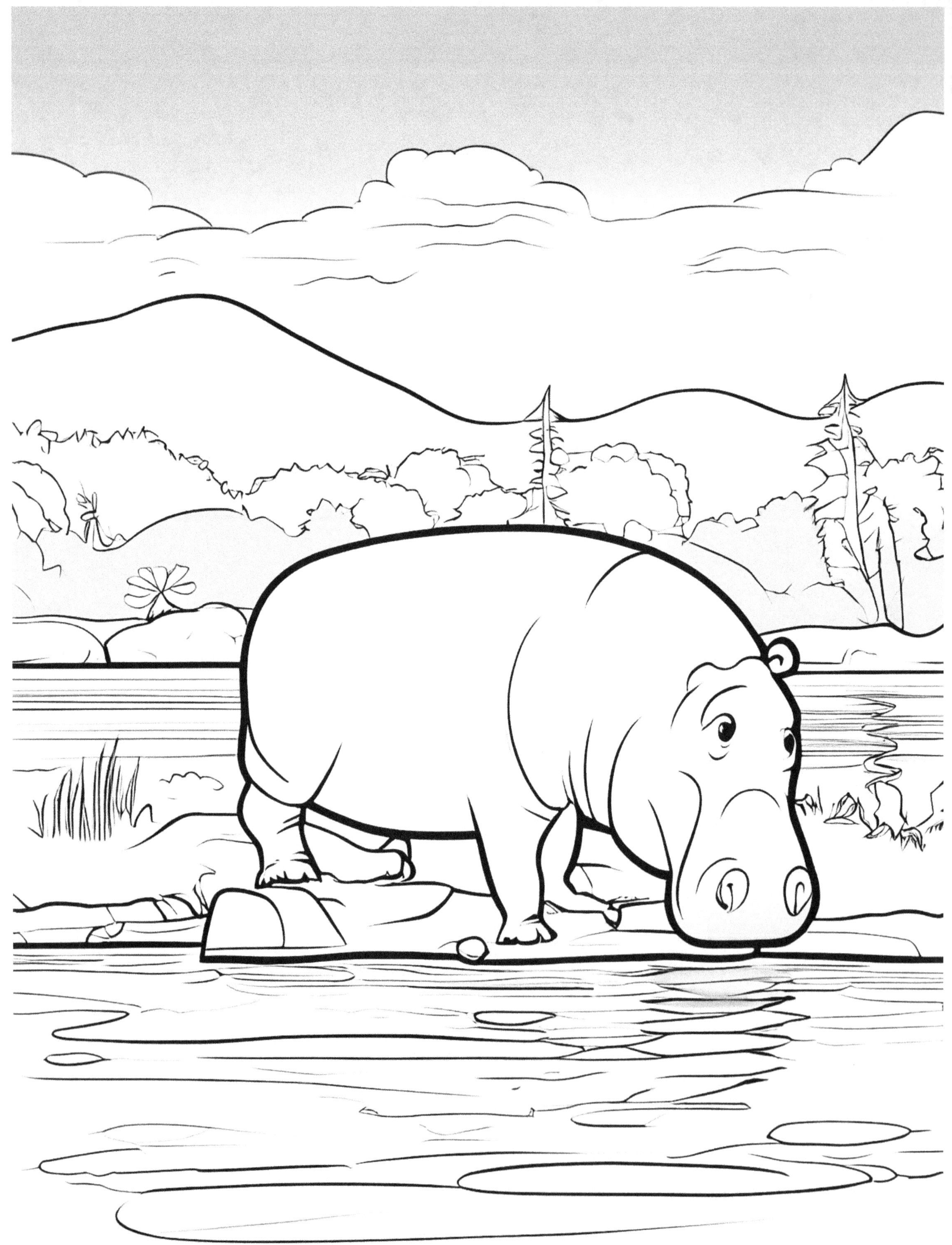

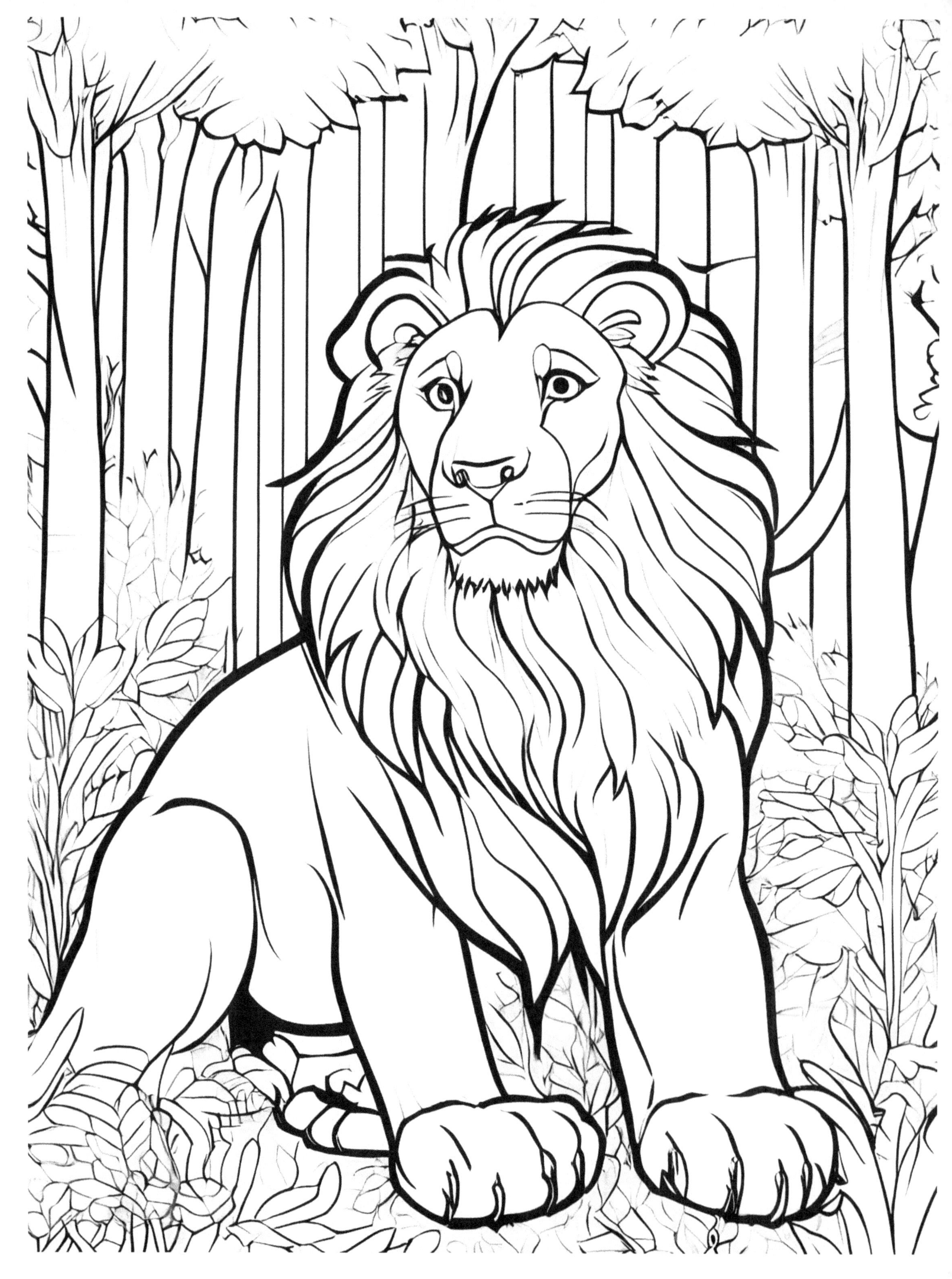

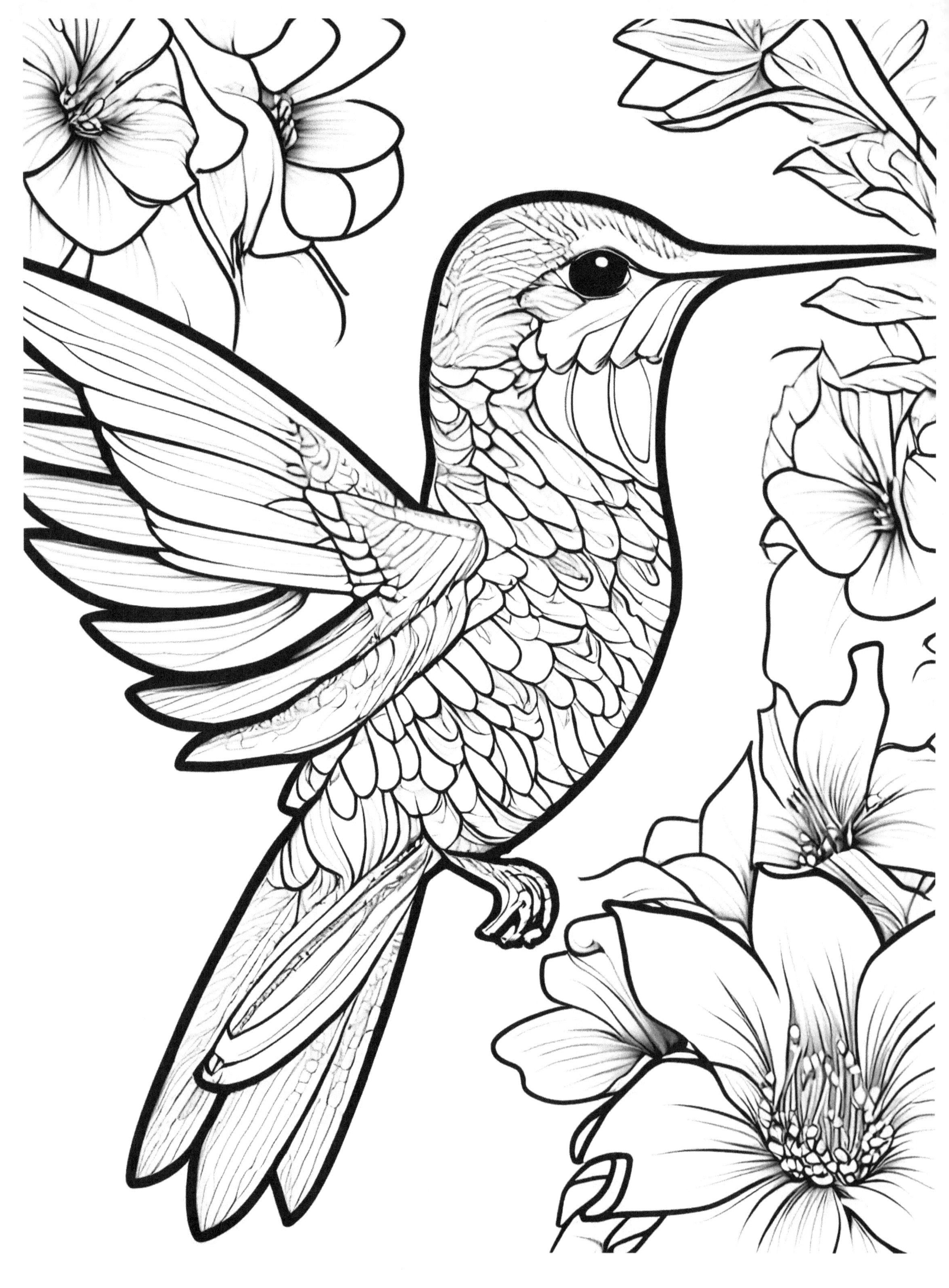

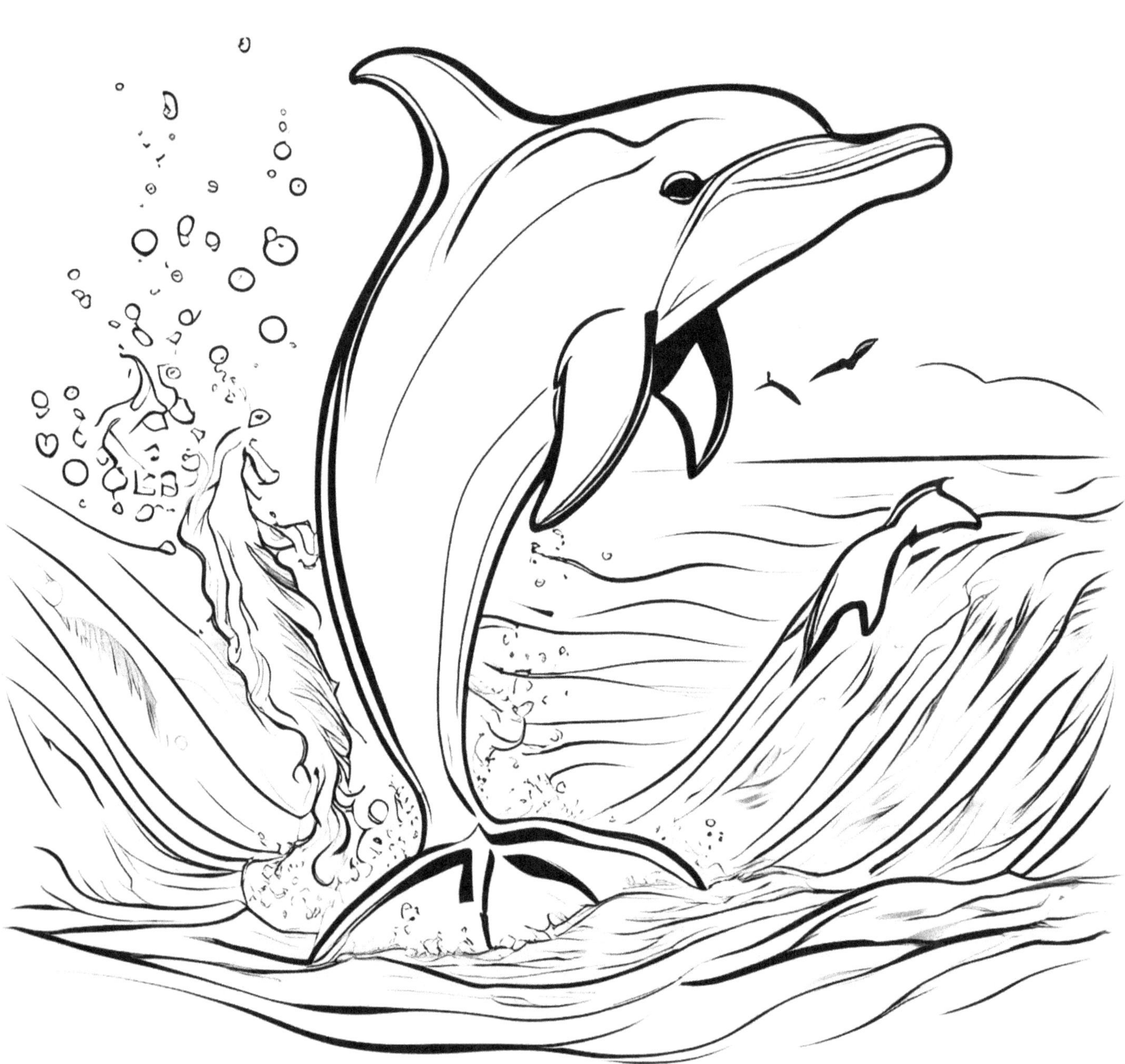

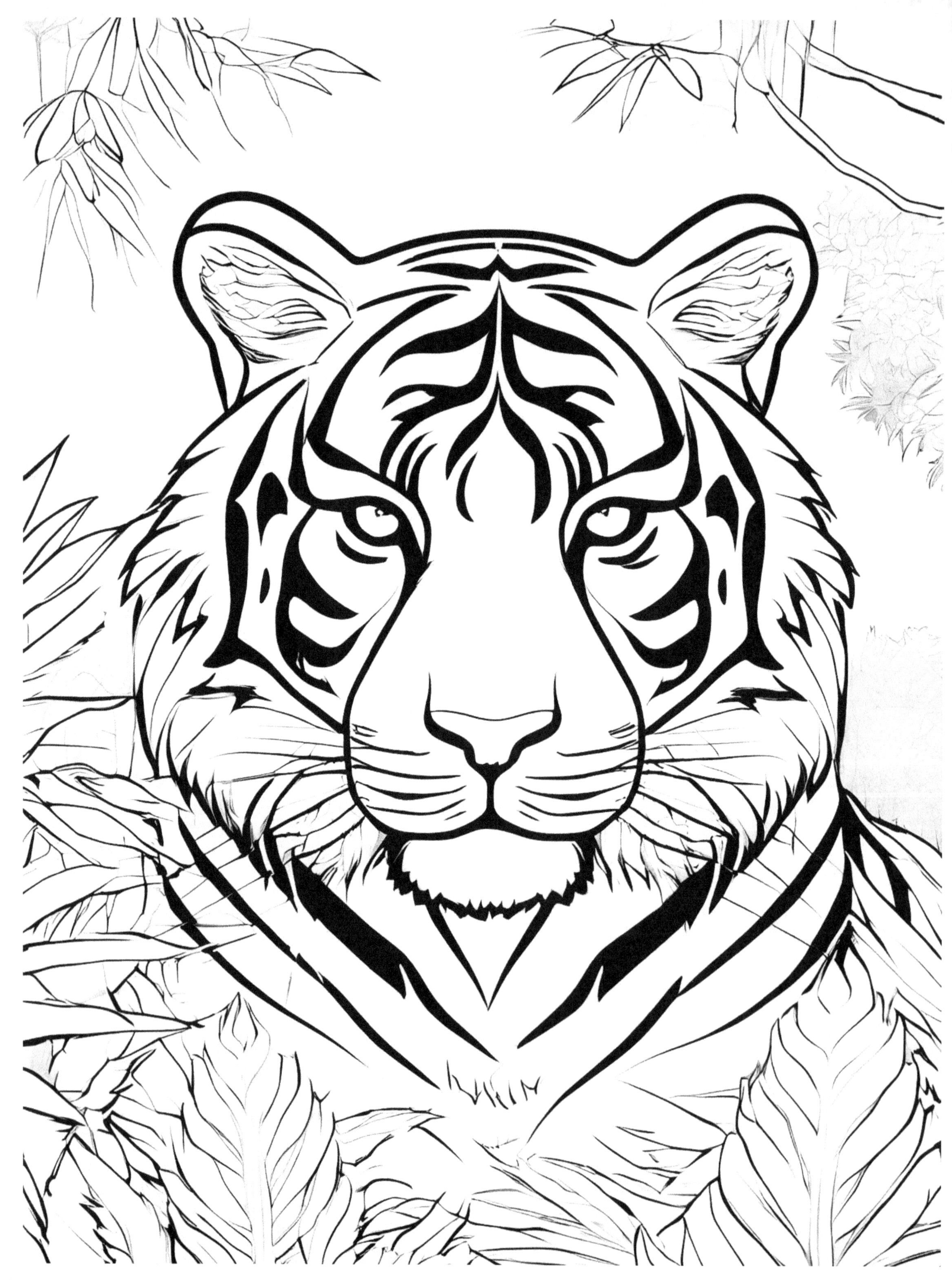

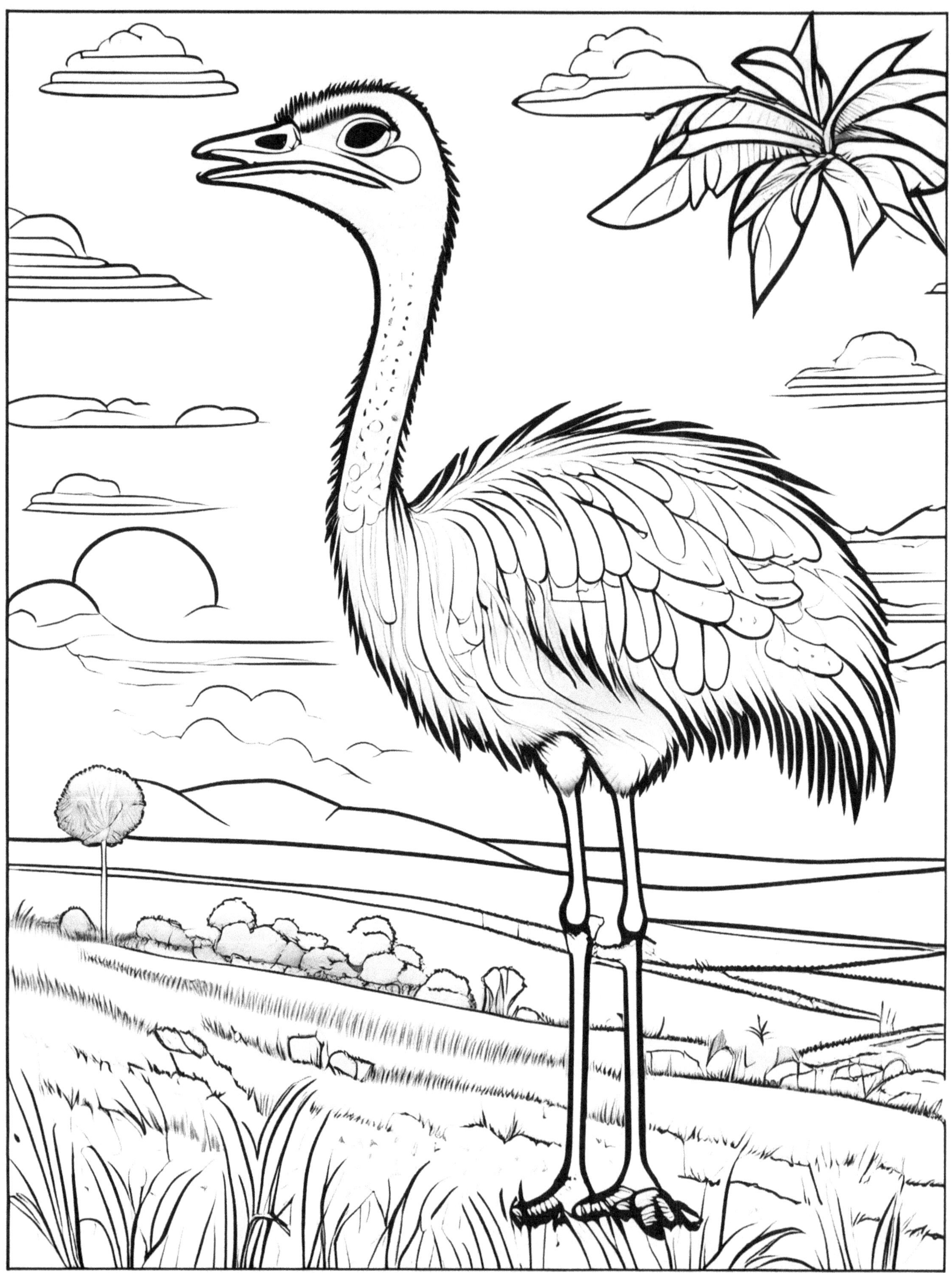

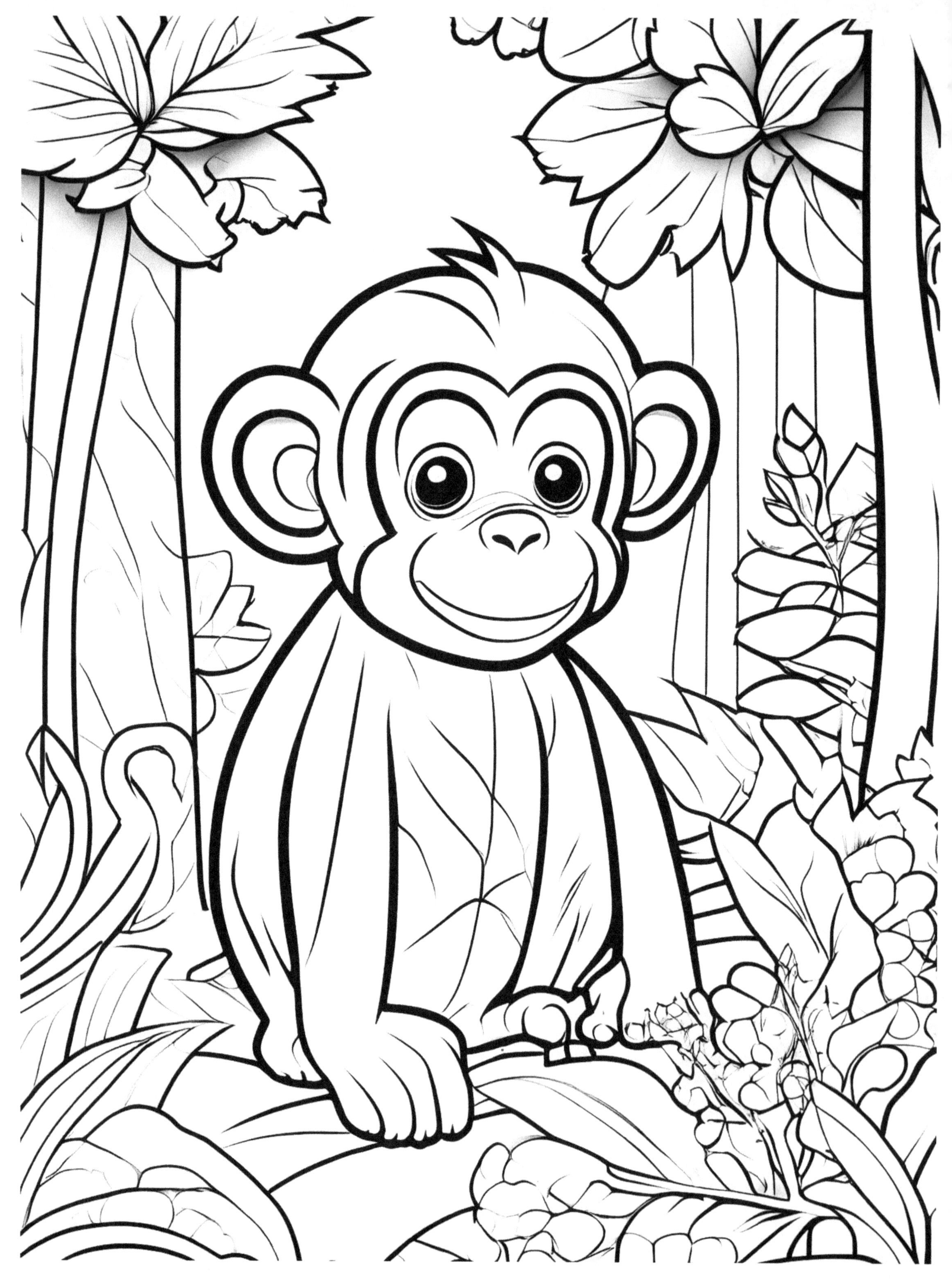

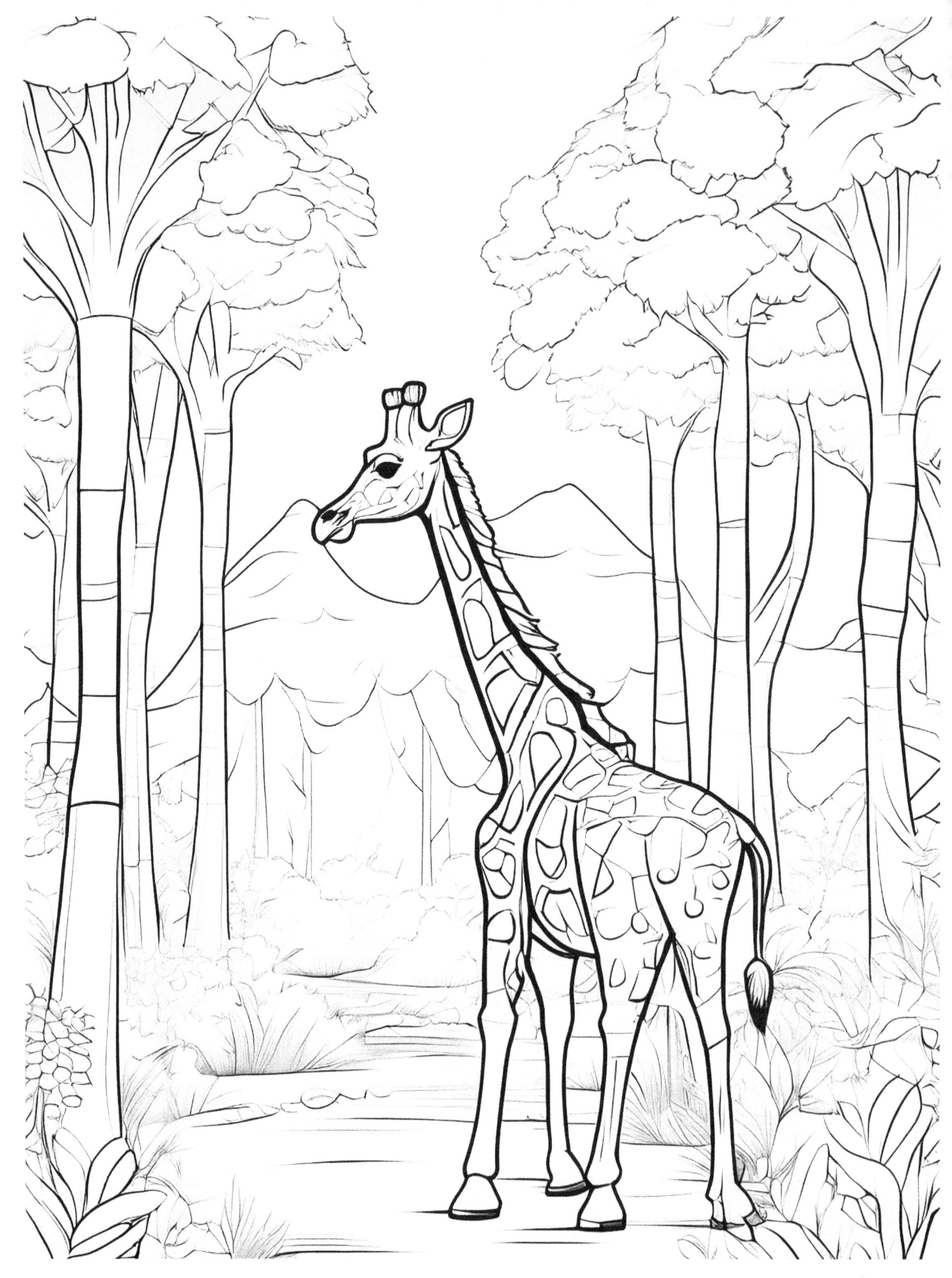

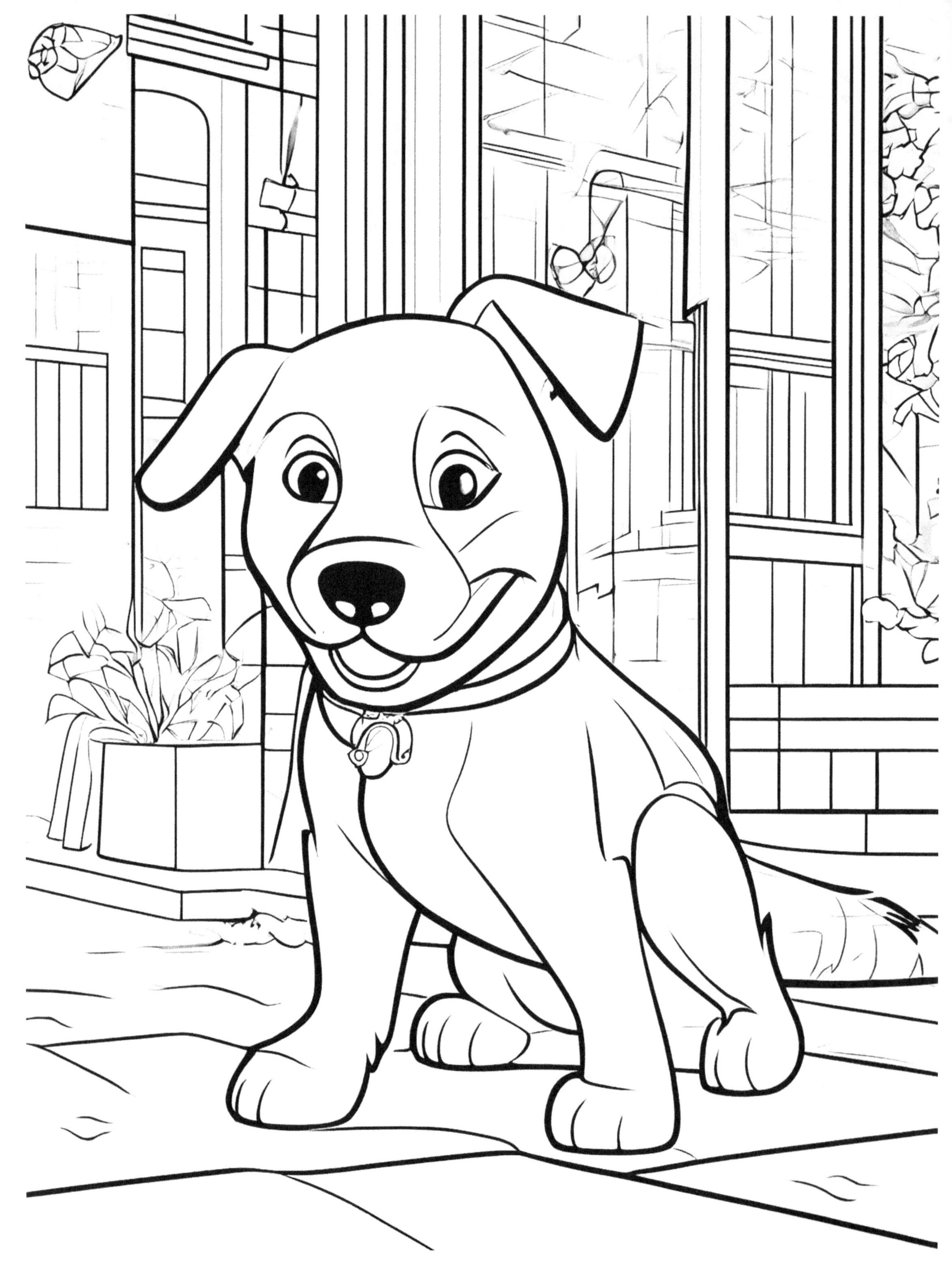

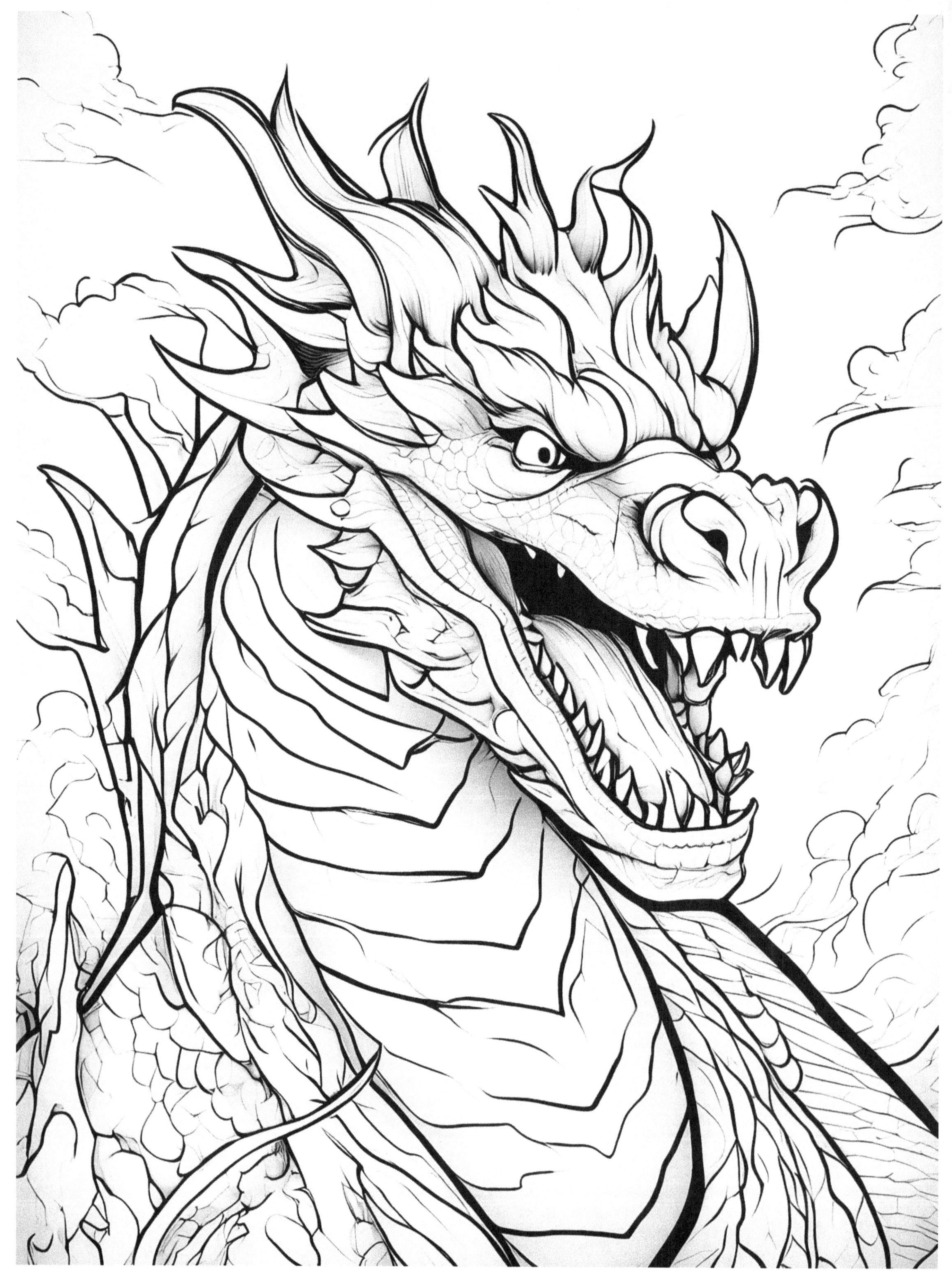

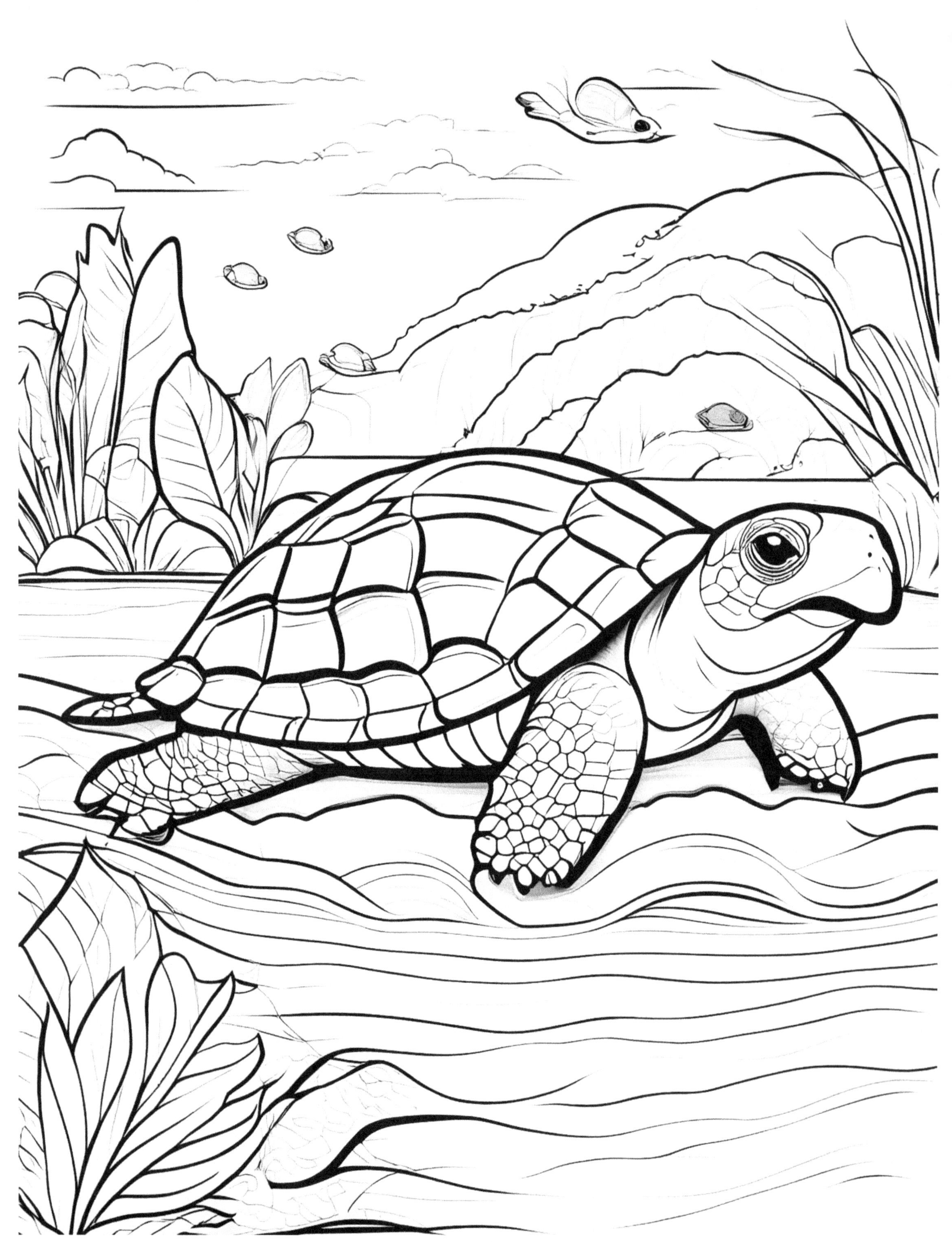

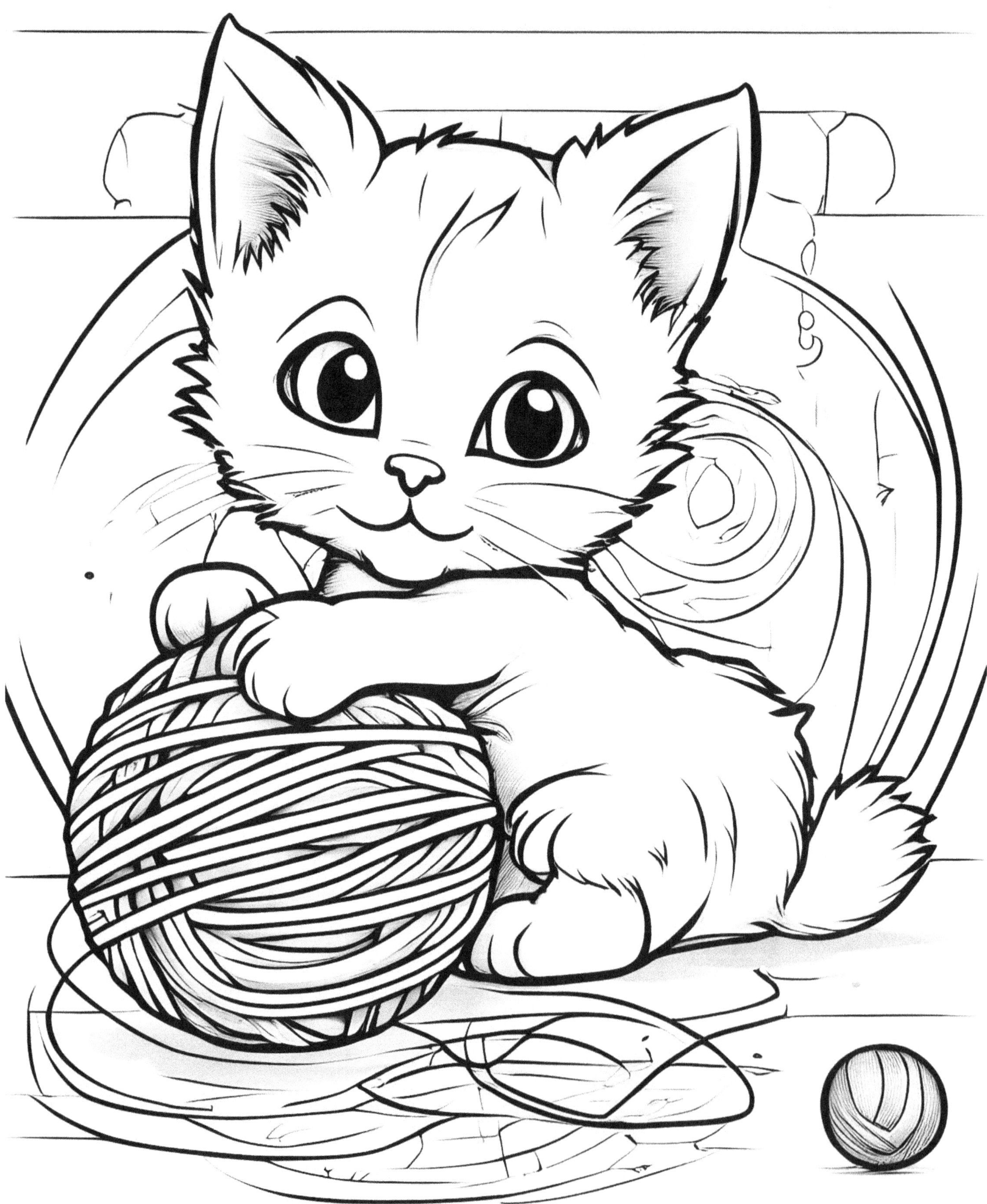

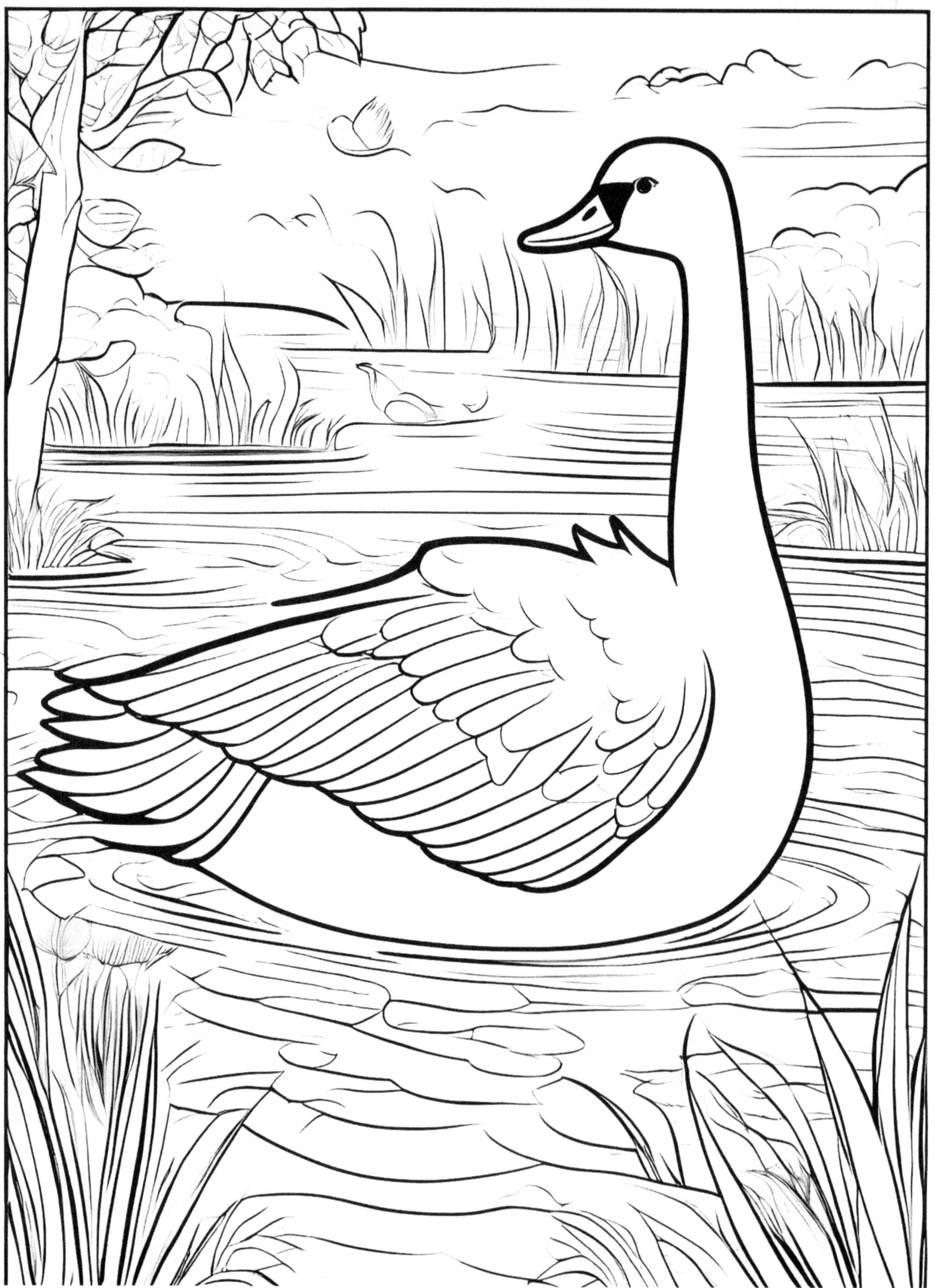

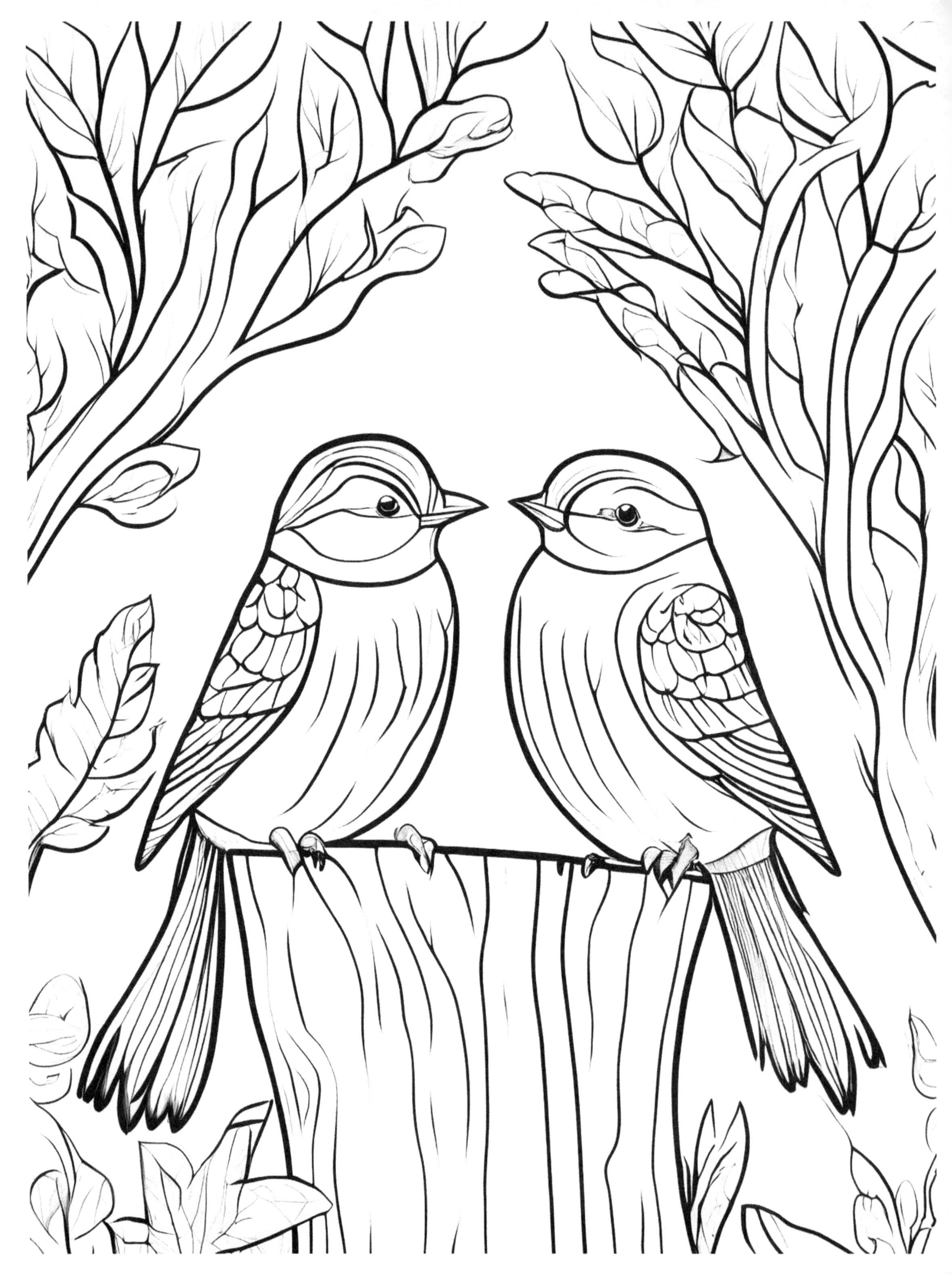

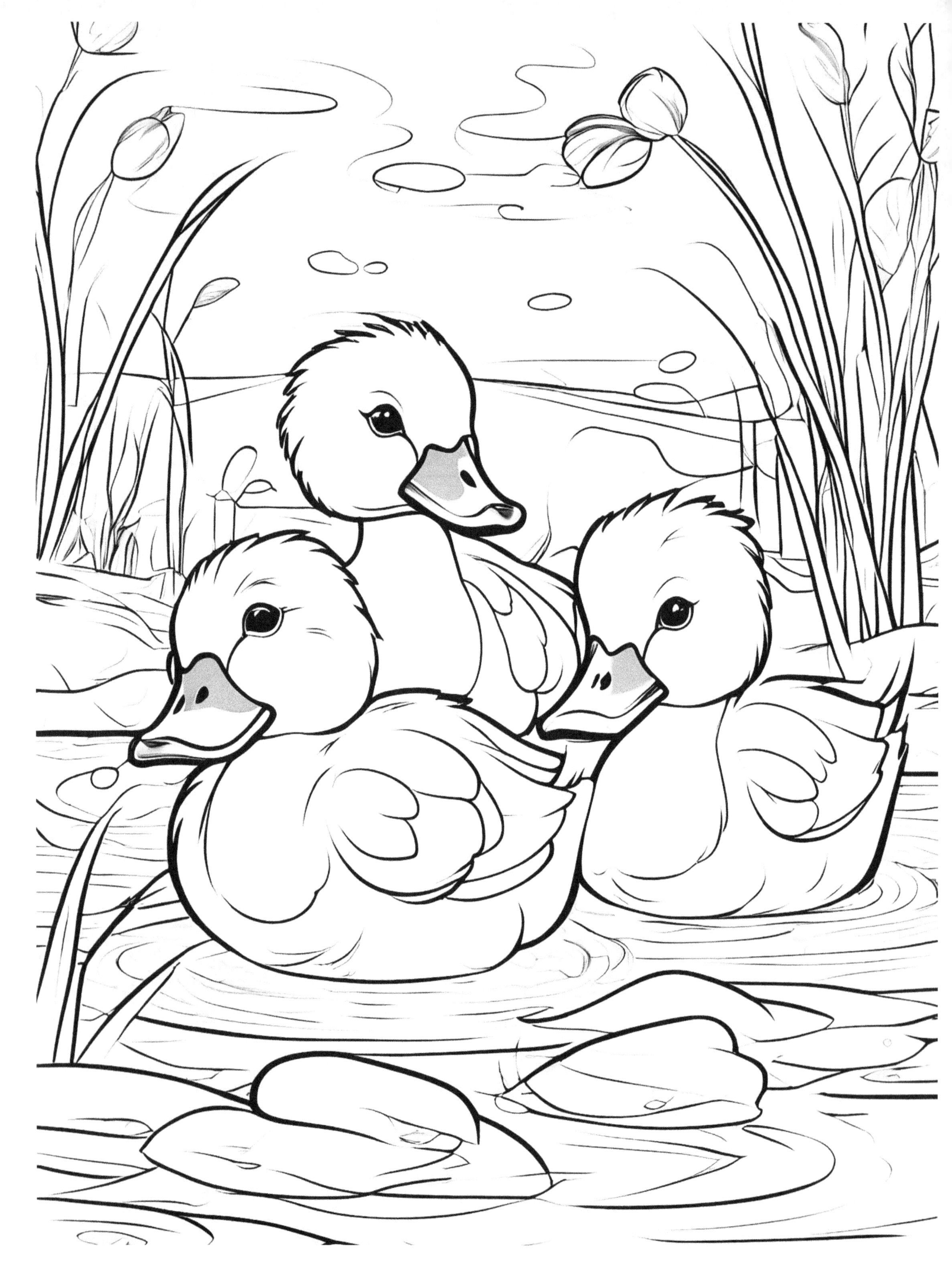

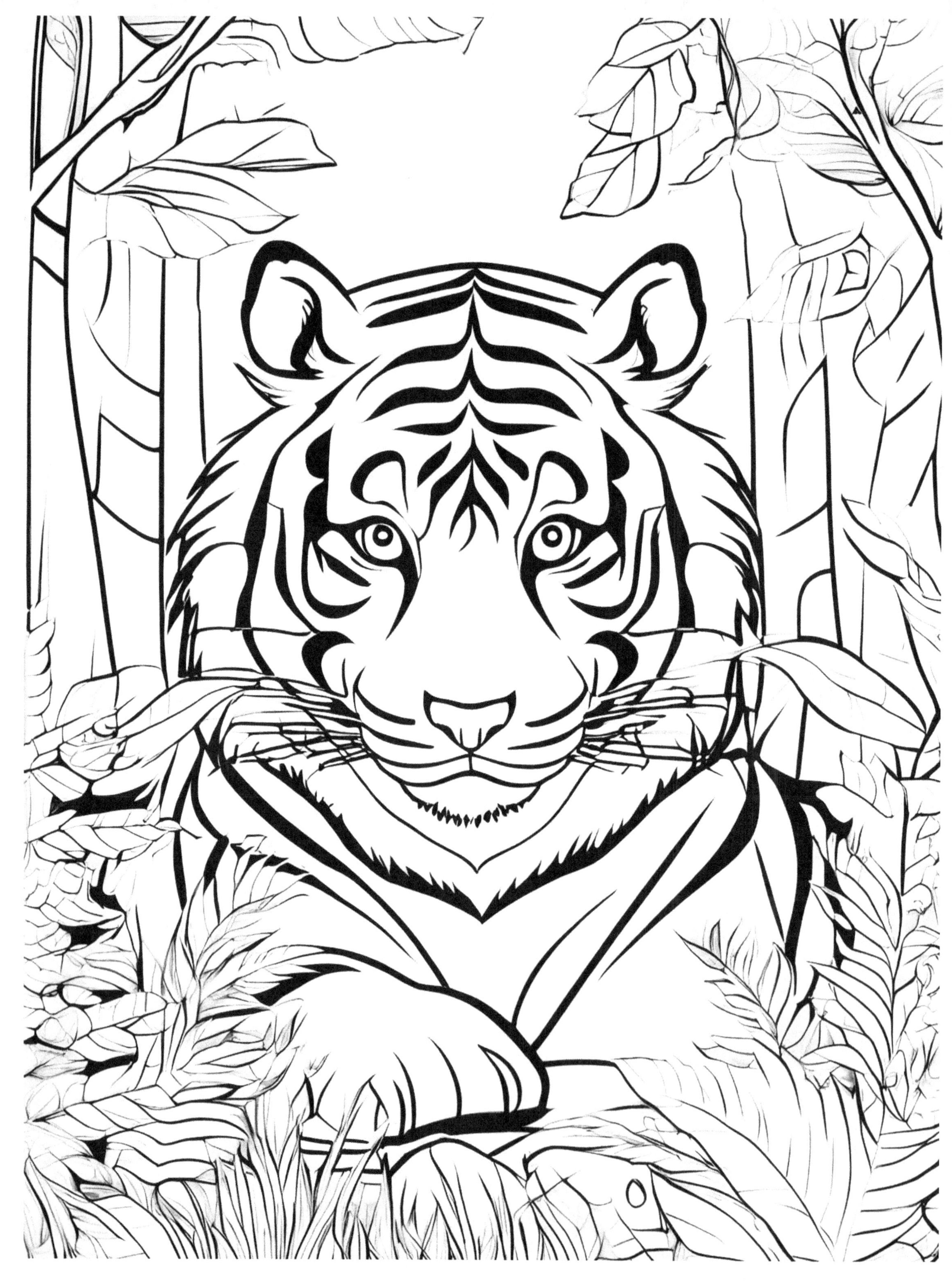

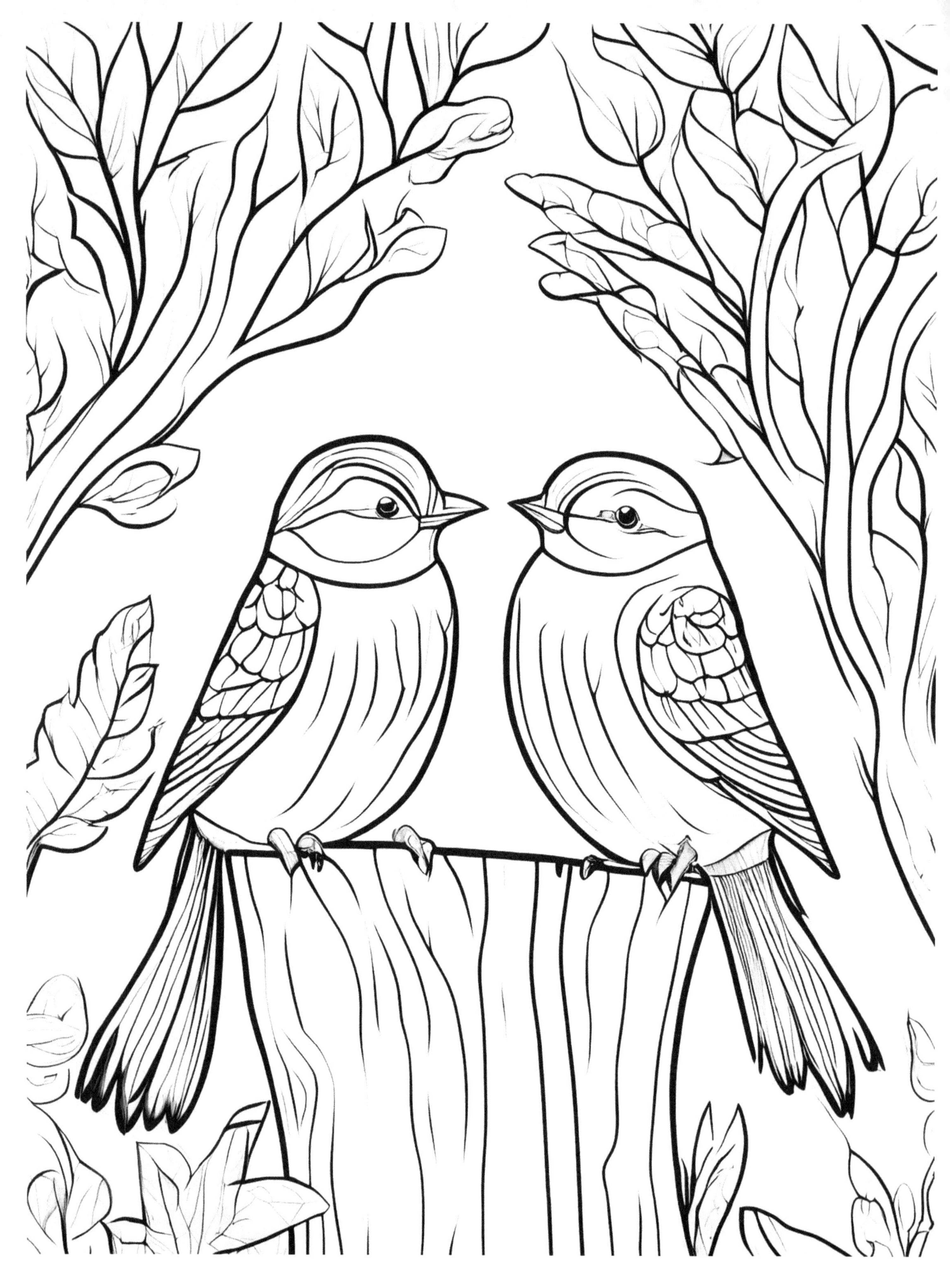

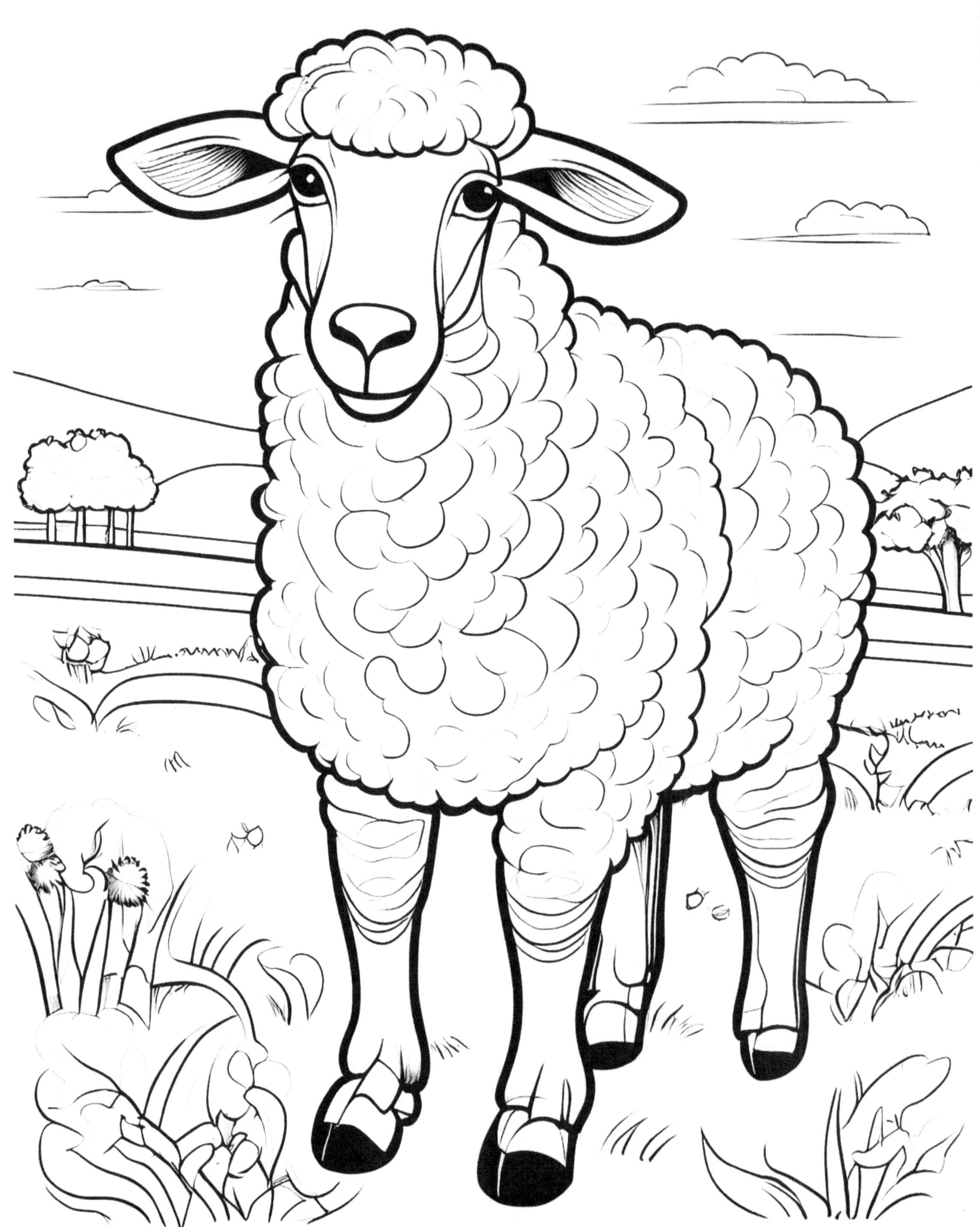

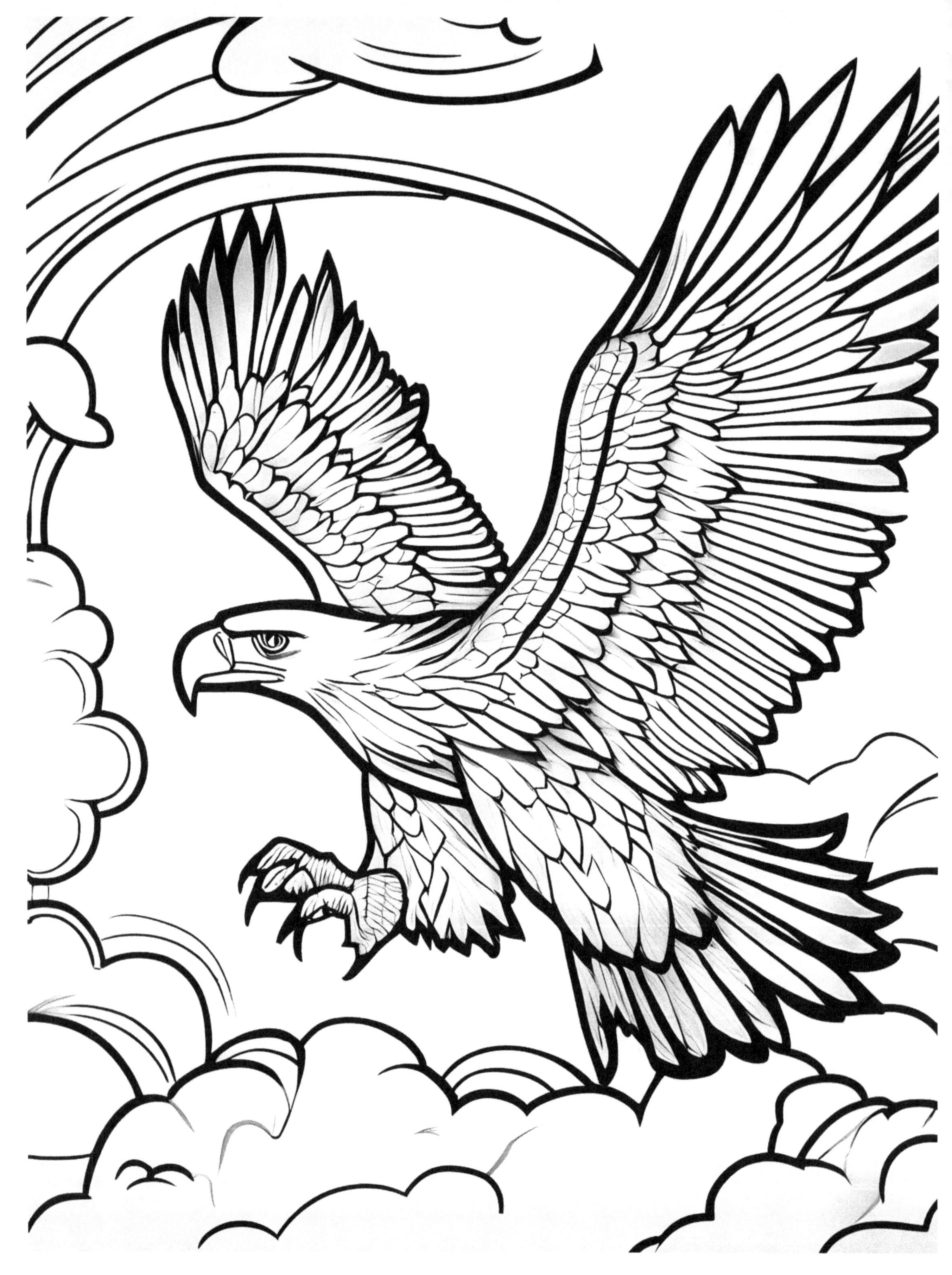

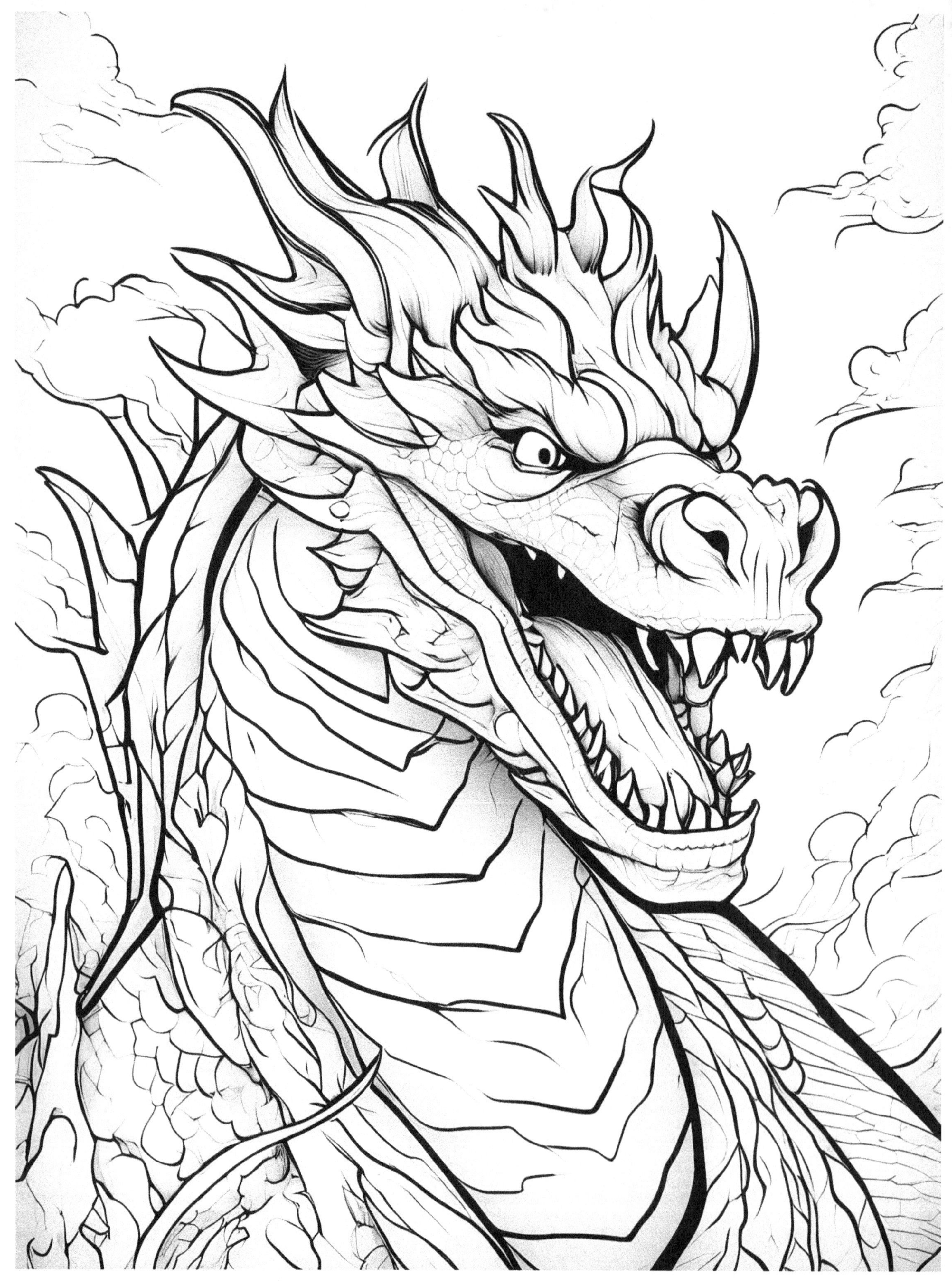

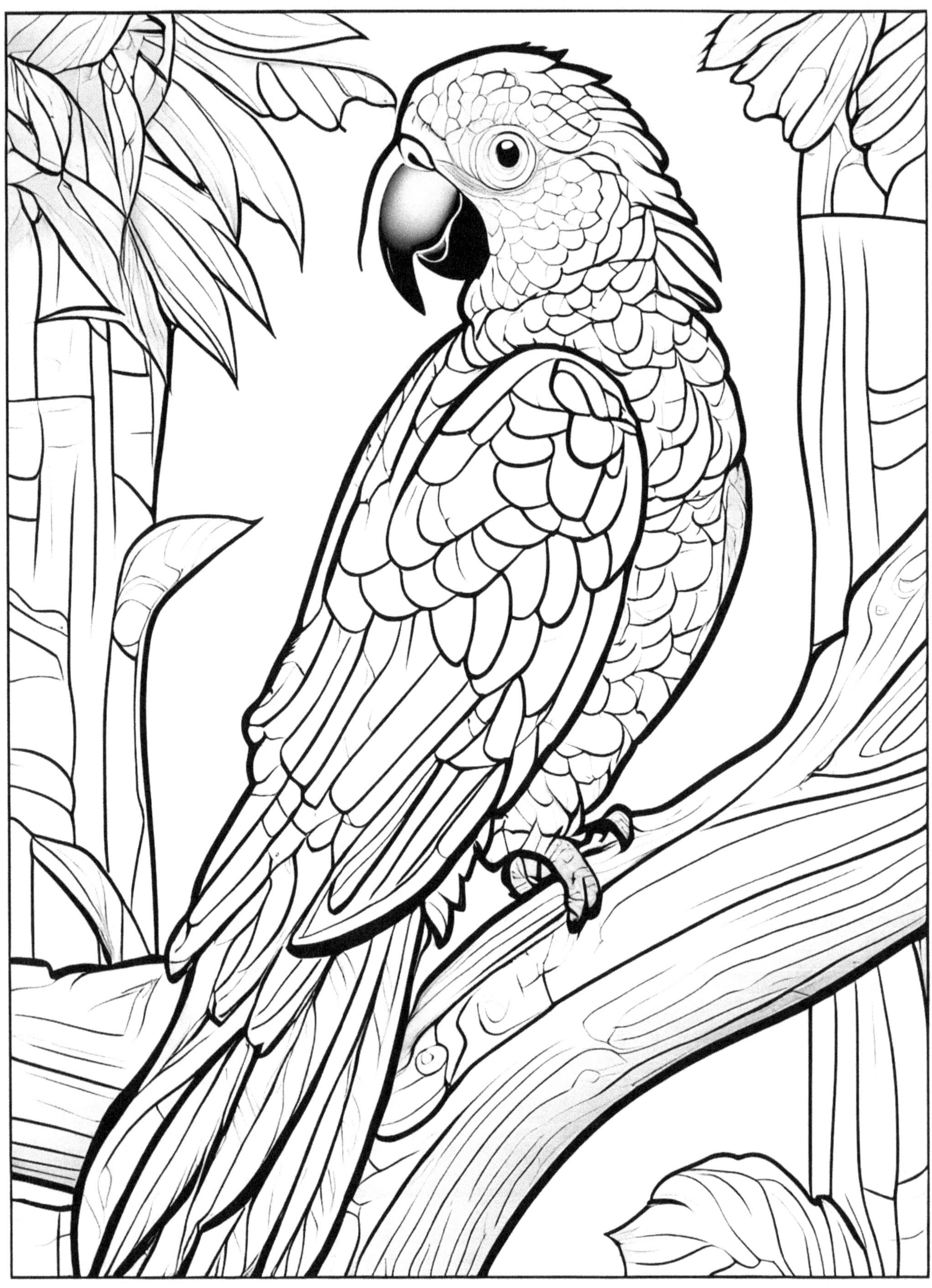

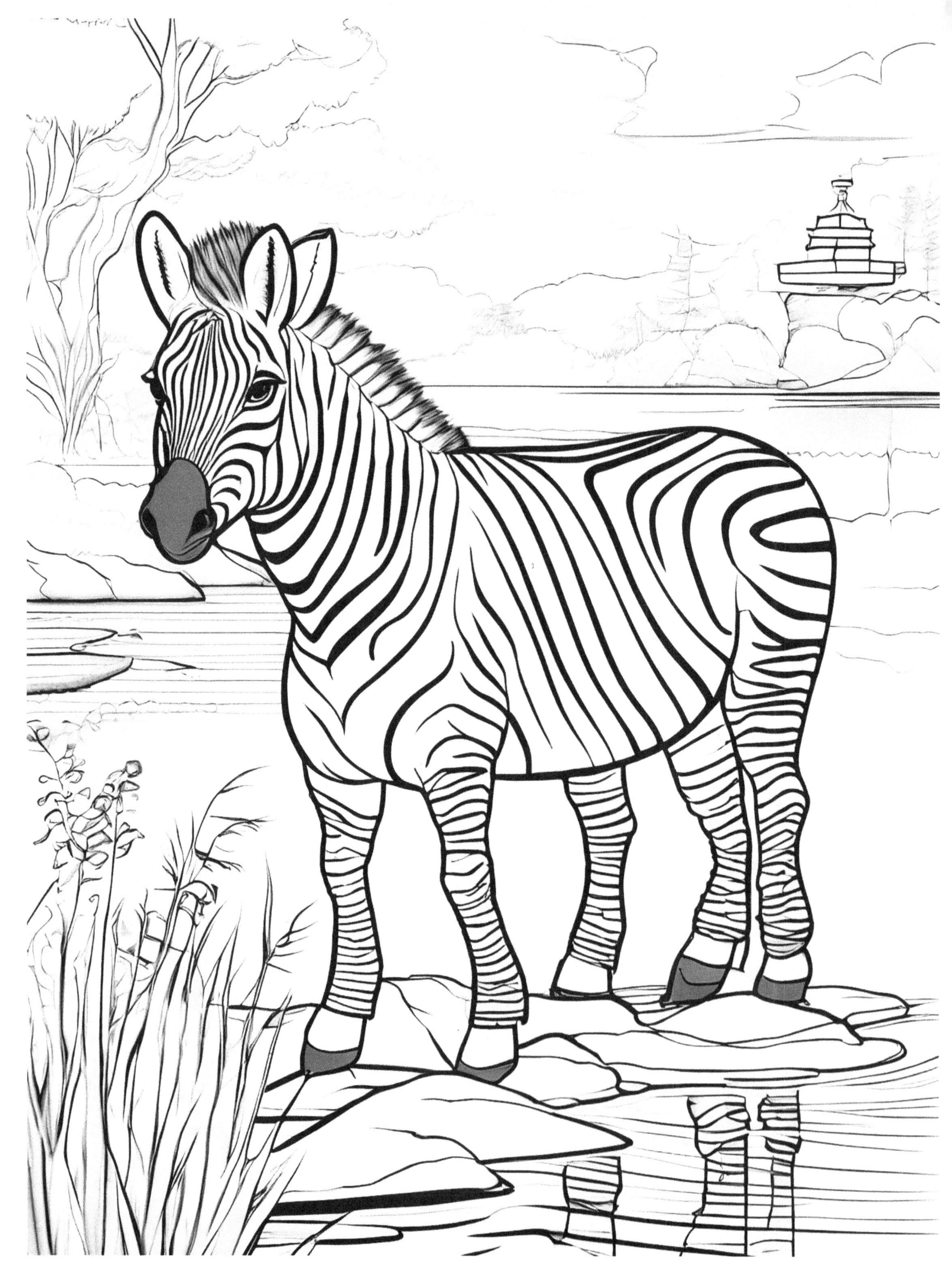

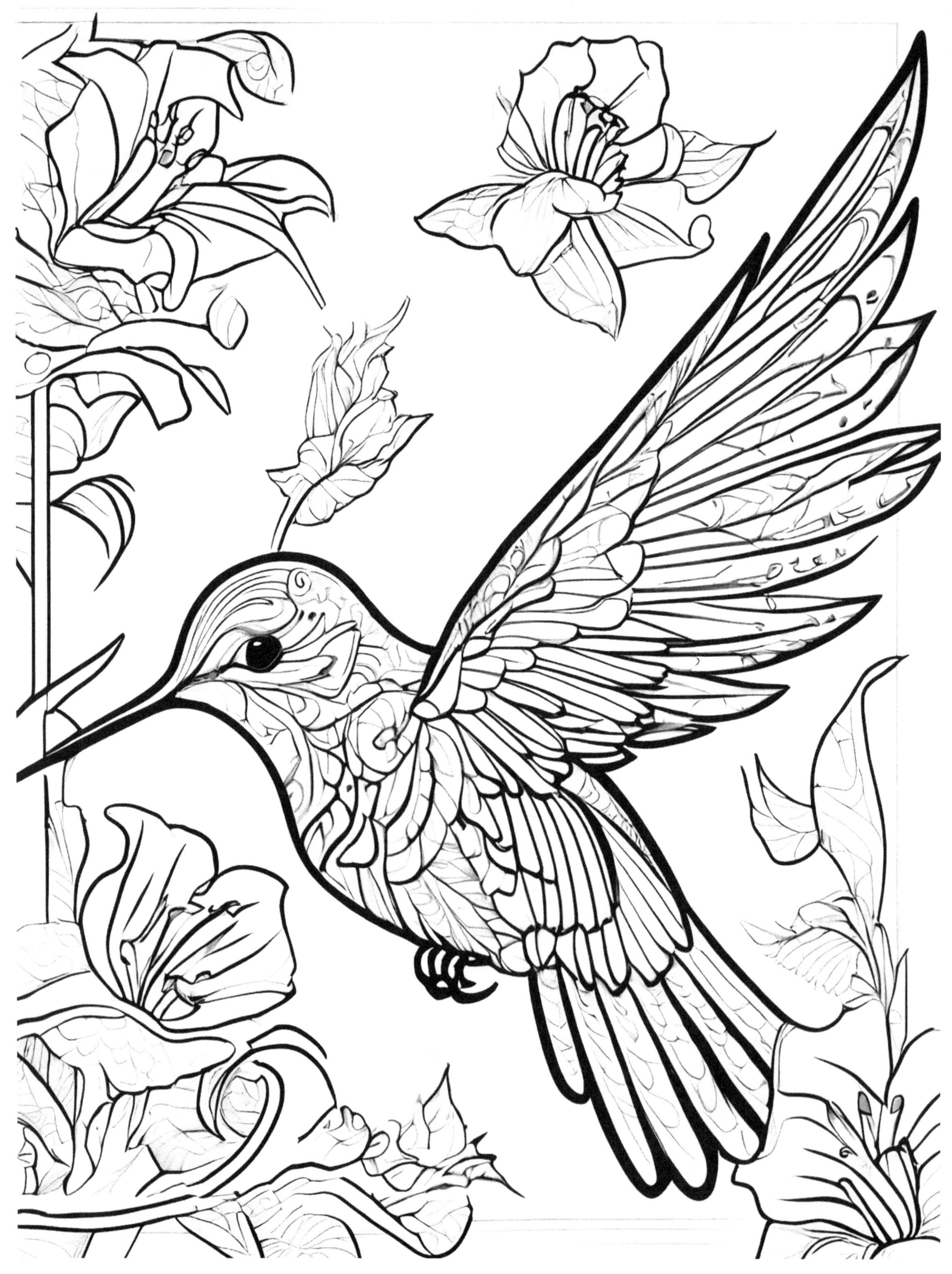

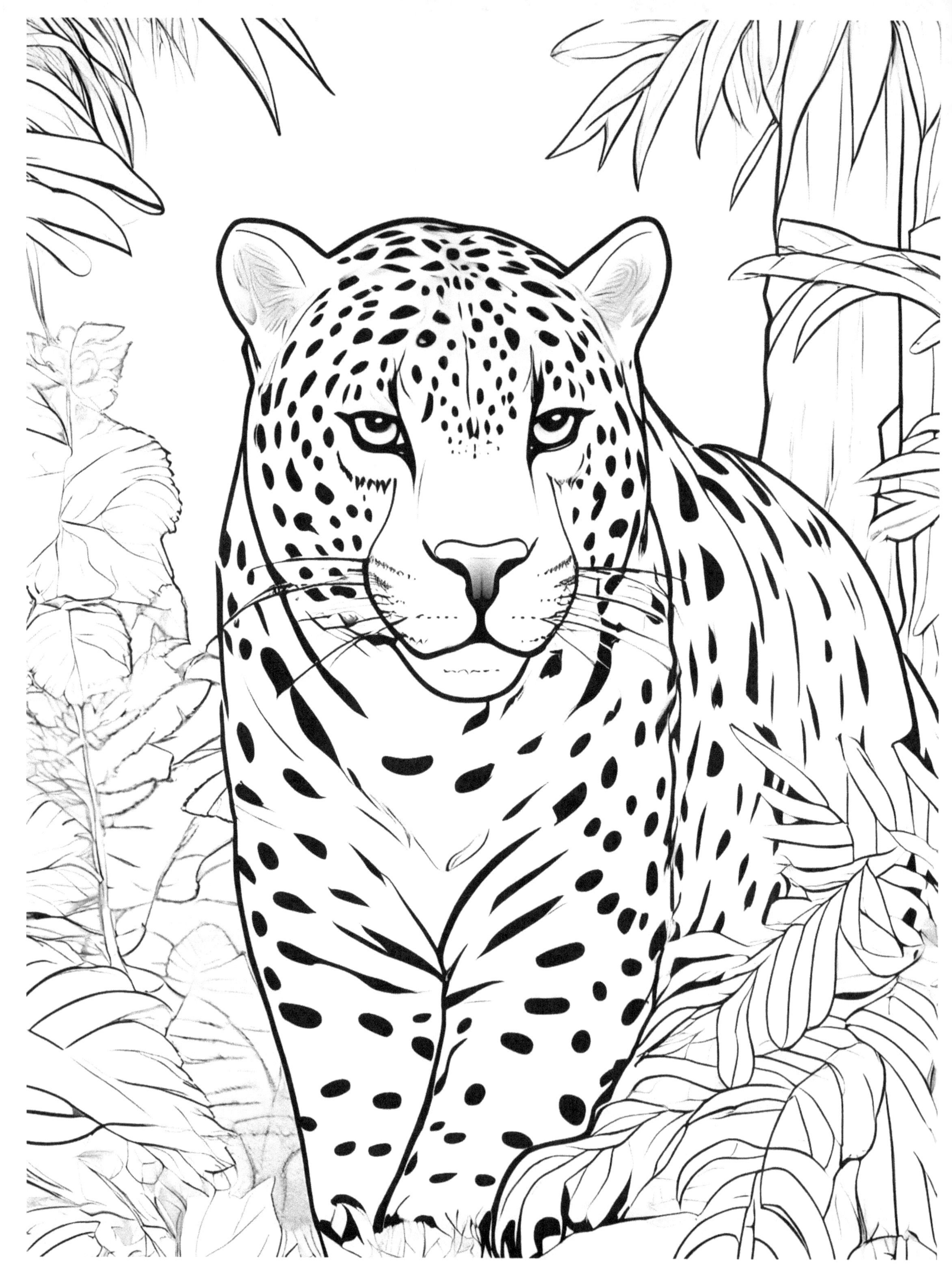

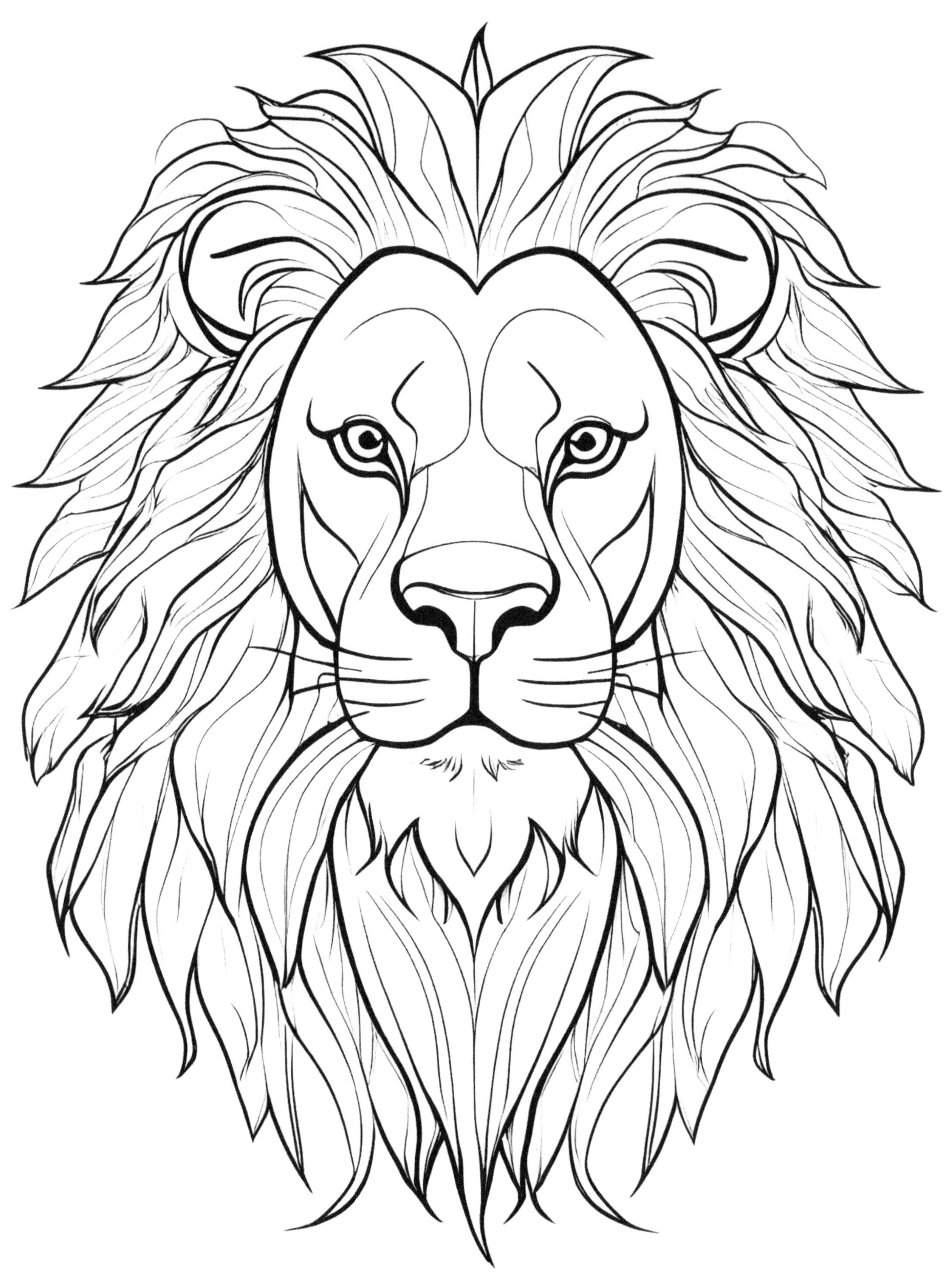

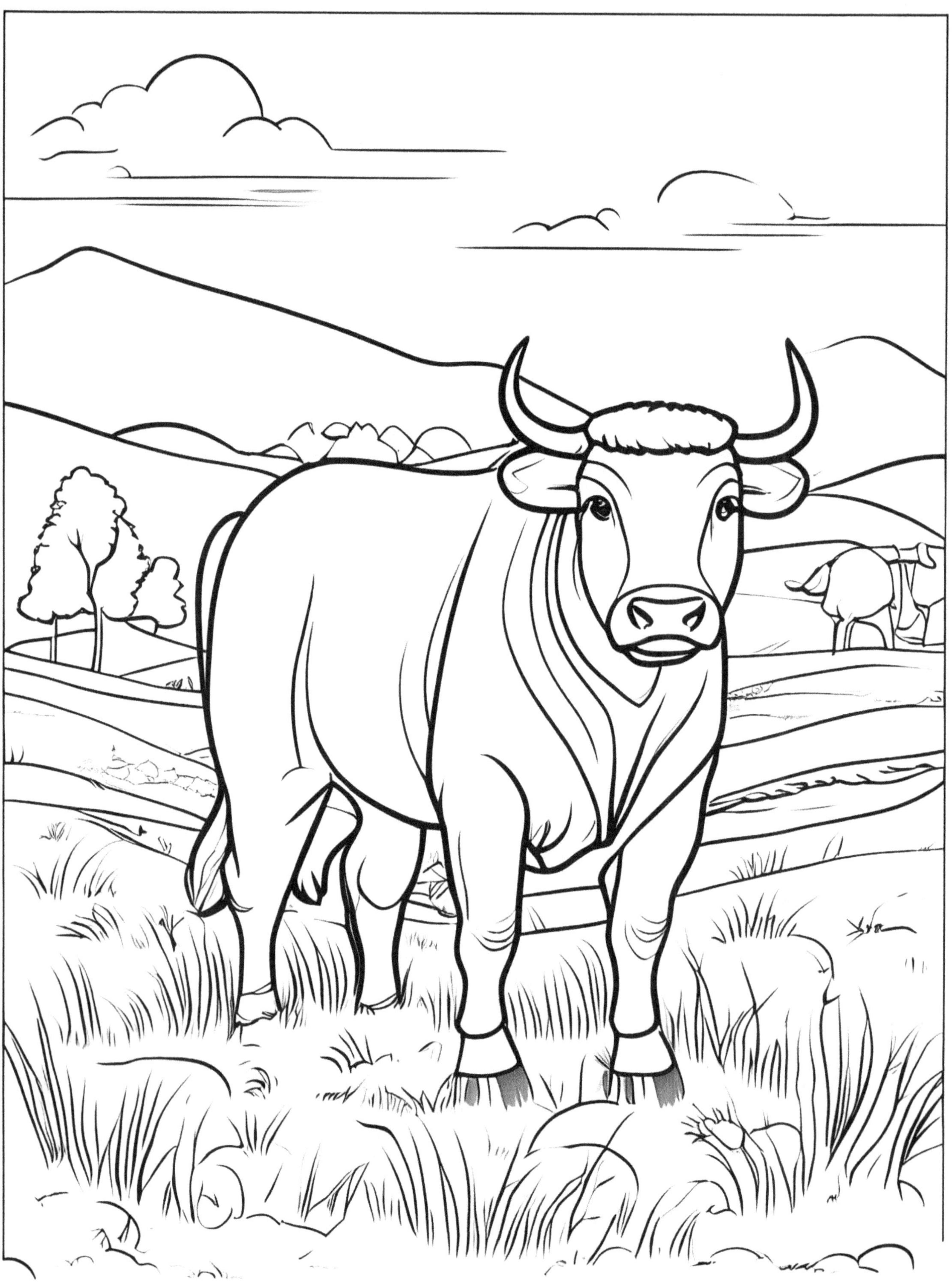

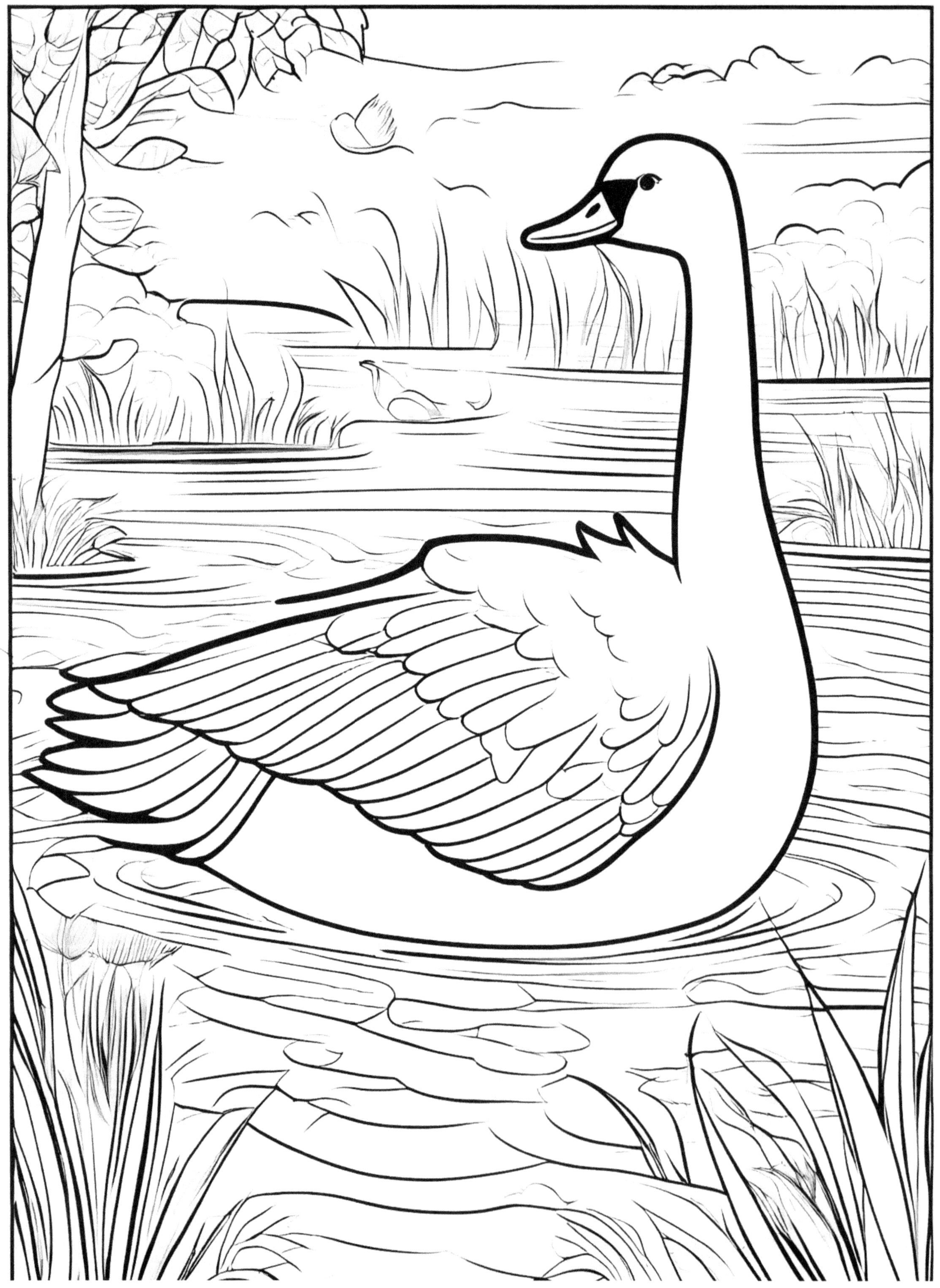

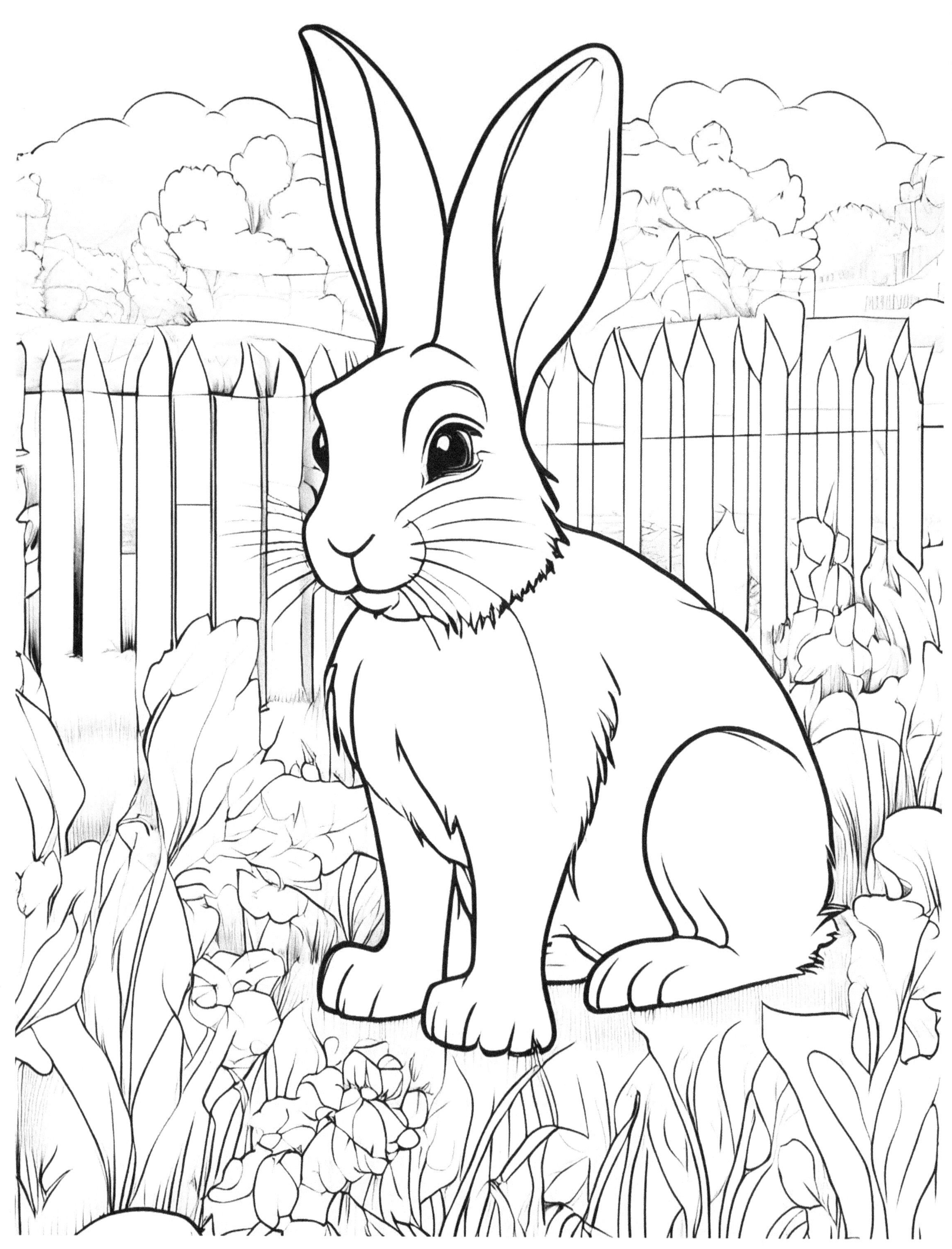